BE EXTRAORDINARY

Boost your ability to truly live a life filled with inner peace, love, integrity and joy by mastering three simple steps that great teachers, masters and gurus have been using for centuries to empower themselves.

Not having full control over our minds and emotions is a significant source of human suffering. Learning how to have this control will enhance your ability to be happier and profoundly more peaceful in the now.

Easily dissolve stress, fear and worry by learning how to dramatically and permanently shift your perspective.

D1602238

Review

"I loved it! It is clear, funny, engaging, honest and totally real, and can be helpful to so many. Mahima put profound realizations in a simple and accessible way that is practical and down to earth."

Krishna

A Rebel's Guide to Inner Peace

Copyright © 2013 by Mahima Lucille Klinge

Email: hello@lovesilence.com

Website: www.lovesilence.com

ISBN: 978-3-9524190-0-7

First Edition, 2013

Cover and layout : Pri-Ya N. Chen , Mahima L. Klinge

Photography by: Manuel Fischer, Freshpixel Fotostudio

A Rebel's Guide to Inner Peace

"Live The Moment"

Mahima Lucille Klinge

LOVE
SILENCE

Acknowledgements

I would like to thank the following people for their generosity in helping me give birth to this book. Krishna and Andy, thank you both so much for your wonderful input. Lynn Cross thank you for your brilliant proofreading, working with you was such a delight. Priya Chen you are a truly amazing lady! Thank you for helping me create the cover and for designing the book layout. Your tireless efforts are deeply appreciated. To Sebastian Witte for brilliantly transforming my words into German – you rocked the translation like you rock all that you do! To my amazing husband, Kai, for also helping with the German translation and for your limitless love, support and patience through the writing process. What a journey! I would also love to give special thanks to you, my darling sister, for your unwavering belief in me. I am so proud of the amazing and successful woman you have become. To my good friends Leslie, Heinz, Cornelia, Sarlo, Leonardo, Laura and Chantal – I value your loving support and friendship.

Dedication

This book is dedicated to all the people I have ever met and known. Every experience has enriched me, made me grow, made me reflect and made me better. Some of you brought laughter and joy and others tears and pain, but all of you made me stronger, wiser and ultimately, happier, because you helped me to find a love that is limitless and fearless. So, thank you.

Table of Contents

INTRODUCTION

The thick leather belt struck my legs with great force. I was just seven years old. The sound of its repetitive landing was almost as awful as the sharp, stinging pain. I could scream, sob or plead, but there was no escaping the harsh reality of these abusive discipline tactics. My experiences are not unique to my family nor even especially cruel, according to them. It was the reality of most kids born in my part of the world. And I suspect not much has changed in that neighborhood I was brought up in. One could even say it is the way that people there show their love. Show that they care about you!

What dreadful crime would you need to commit to be subjected to such treatment? It really did not take a whole lot to trigger this kind of reaction. Violence in some form is sadly still a way of life for most people around the world. We don't want to talk too much about it. We even prefer to think that it is only happening on a very small scale, nothing to be too concerned about. Even kids kill now! And yet we still manage to convince ourselves that we are making great progress in our spiritual evolution/revolution. Through our thoughts, feelings and actions, we are creators. We are born with the ability to be beautiful, and we are also given the choice to be terrible! I hope to shine a floodlight on the urgency, importance and tremendous value of individual self-exploration and self-development.

We need to seriously move away from the group mentality, which has damaging limitations. Instead of fitting in, maybe it's time to gracefully rebel and stand out.

Three wonderfully simple, essential and fundamental steps to connecting to inner peace in the now are contained in these pages. If you are looking to enhance your ability to feel more connected to peace, love, compassion and happiness in your everyday life, then you have picked up the right book.

We all have the potential to be empowered, to wake up and to be enlightened, because it is our birthright. It is not something special, elite and unreachable, bestowed upon a chosen few. This is just another shameful misdirection to keep control and manipulate us into being followers rather than blossoming into leaders. Remember, leading is not just about leading other people – it's just as much about leading ourselves. Leading ourselves out of a life of unawareness. If we do this, we become a great inspiration to others.

Do not let the achievements of others distract you or make you believe that happiness and real greatness is an impossible goal for you. We don't all need to become a Mother Teresa or a Dalai Lama to greatly affect the world and inspire the people around us. I come from the "keep it simple" school of philosophy and aspire to this – bringing my best attitude to each moment. I give my full heart to everything that I do. Even the simple mundane tasks of life can be performed with the greatest care, heart and attention to detail. That's what makes life become a continuous celebration. A dance with divinity. A sacred pilgrimage, if I can connect to deep joy, profound love and peace in the now. Do trust me when I tell you that anyone else who really wants to can do the same. It's not a spiritual gift passed onto you by higher forces, it is a personal choice you make new each moment.

Peace belongs to us all. It is the DNA of our souls. We just need to focus on it again, open up to it again...

And again...

And again...

And again, until being peaceful and spreading joy becomes as effortless as blinking, because it is so much a part of who you are, what you do and how you live your daily life. Silence is the key to

Introduction

your inner freedom and personal strength. Integrity is the door that key opens to reveal your loving self. I took a quantum leap out of my mind and into my heart and crash-landed in the now. Let me share what I have learnt thus far.

PEACE IS A CHOICE

Where is our focus? We do have the power to influence our outside reality greatly through the choices we make and where we choose to put our focus.

Self-awareness will help you understand yourself better through noticing what kinds of thoughts pass through your mind and what emotions you indulge in. Self-awareness will allow you to shift your focus from the negative to the positive.

I learnt to make better choices when I was very tired of my own personal suffering. Suffering that came from an inability to stop thinking negatively. Suffering that came from holding on to my past and fretting about my future. So when I discovered a way out of that, boy, did I pay attention! When I first tasted freedom from the endless negativity of my mind and emotions, I knew I had happened upon a life-changing experience that I would honor deeply and keep focused on until my last breath.

I would like to break down some of the more complex spiritual philosophies into a straightforward language that many more people can relate to than do now. The three steps I will focus on in this book are . . .

1. Finding out who we are beyond the body and mind.

2. Realizing and practicing unconditional love.

3. Connecting to inner peace in the now.

To find happiness in this world, you will first have to find it within. To find love, you will first have to experience its power in your own heart. To find peace, you will first have to know your own peace. The more powerful the connection you have to your inner joy, love and peace, the better choices you will make and the easier the outer dance of life becomes.

LIVING IN THE NOW

Life is similar to an illusion in a magic show. It appears to be so real, but it is really just a trick. In this case, life is a trick of the mind. The additional illusion of "thinking we have time" blinds us further into believing the illusion is real. What do I mean by "life is an illusion"? When you wake up every morning and have to get dressed and go to work, it feels real enough, right? Some dreams also feel very real until you wake up and realize, "Oh, thank God! It was just a dream". Or, on the contrary, you may wish it had been real and not just a dream! Fact is, the stay in the body is temporary and the time we have unknown. This means that death would be a sudden waking up from this dream state, which we prefer to call "life". Which means that life is very much a dream from which you die and wake up from.

The cool thing about waking up from a dream is that everything that was going on in that dream stops. So if you were terrified in the dream, you wake up and stop being terrified. You feel relieved. If you were running in the dream, you stop running the moment you wake up. So it can be said that dying would definitely wake you up from this dream that we call life. Somehow we know intuitively that death would be some kind of a relief. That's why some people choose that option when the going gets too tough to bear. However, I have a much better suggestion to stop the emotional suffering from even getting to such an extreme point. Wake up to the now. The effect is the same. When you wake up to the now, you see clearly how time is a dangerous illusion that can rob you of your appreciation of life itself. Wake up from the time illusion and you will see this: you came into this world with nothing, and no matter what happens in the meantime, you will leave with the same – nothing. You may wonder what all the fuss is about. Why are we fighting, scraping, losing ourselves in intense emotions and endless desires? A good question indeed! Know this: it's all just a dream, an experience that has a beginning – birth, and an end – death. Just wake up to the now. It would all be a lot easier if we would refrain from taking ourselves so seriously and making ourselves so important. You are a character in a dream. Accepting this will free up energy and stop you from suffering unnecessarily.

What do we really know about life? We would be wise to use what little we do know to empower ourselves. The physical body will die one day. We know this for sure – right now, at least. Who knows where science will take us in the future? But for today, our death is a fact. We don't know when, why or how it will happen, but we know death of the body is certain. It is one of the truths that every single human being shares. I hope this truth helps you to start to having a new appreciation for the now. It is so clear that all we have for sure is this moment.

This is your life right now. This is you right now. The rest is just good and bad memories from the past, hopes and dreams for the future. The reality is that your life has an expiration date. Most of us are born without remembering what that date is. I personally feel good about that fact. At any given moment you could wake up from this "dream life" through death, like so many people leaving their bodies right now as you are reading these very words. People, young and old, rich and poor, all over the world, are united by the truth of death. They are waking up from the "dream" we call life.

The good news is that you don't necessarily need to die to wake up from this dream. Incorporate this philosophy of dying into the philosophy of how you live now. You don't know how much time you have to live, to love, to laugh and to breathe. Wisdom would be waking up to that powerful truth and giving great importance to learning the art of living in the now. Are you waiting for something important to happen in your life so you can start to be happy and truly start living? Are you waiting for a wedding, a promotion, an academic achievement or a large sum of cash? Your dream job, the perfect place to live? Whatever our current reality is, we should wait for nothing and no one to release our joy into this world, because while we wait for change to bring happiness, precious years of our lives are being lost forever.

Be the best you can be in the here and now, and fully embrace the gift we take for granted – life itself. Without life and a body to experience the world through, is there really any point to all this madness and chaos life can appear to be? Without life itself, the house you worked hard to pay for might just as well be a sand castle on the beach. Without life itself, the bachelor's degree that you gave up every pleasure to achieve may just as well be used as fancy wallpaper. Do not lose your ability to laugh, be playful, kind, and feel deep contentment just to own a house in a "dream world". Receive life with open arms and full awareness of each new moment as it is happening and unfolding. Have the courage to do only that which brings joy to your heart. Do not underestimate the importance of your positive attitude, high spirits and enthusiasm to live. It's a gift to the world around you. Each day you have to breathe, you can create something special, joyful and loving around you. It does not matter how poor or rich you are – this moment, like death, doesn't care about that. It offers empowerment to all those who seek its truth. Being in the now is freedom from the suffering of the past and also freedom from the fear and uncertainty of the future.

MY PERSONAL JOURNEY INTO FREEDOM

Let me take you on a wild ride through my past. I want to share some intimate details on how I became the woman I am today. Along the journey I have gathered many beautiful pearls of wisdom, gifts reaped from navigating life's ocean of calm and chaos! May you read and feel inspired, motivated and liberated to live your life with more peace and contentment in the now.

My life's path could have turned down any number of unfortunate roads had I not had the opportunity to learn some of the knowledge I want to share with you. I discovered the profound intelligence in taking full responsibility for what I create with my actions, words, thoughts and feelings. What we are doing right now is creating our future (a future which may or may not come to pass due to the possible death of the physical body, which we must factor into how we live in the now). So if you are being productive, focused, peaceful, content and enjoying your life, chances are extremely high that your future will be just as bright. If you are abusing your body with too much of the wrong food and drinks or being too negative, angry and confused, chances are high you can look forward to more unpleasant times in the future. Nothing will change until you change, because what we think, feel and do has a direct impact on what happens in our lives. We affect and influence our reality by what we think, feel and do right now. That's why and how people can turn their lives around or make a right mess of it; we are not just victims of fate.

This personal story is a short version of the intriguing road I took to arrive in the now. It is not a full autobiography but rather a glimpse into some important parts of my journey so you can understand better where I come from. I believe we are all born with an enormous potential – a potential we can choose to unleash regardless of where we come from and what has happened to us in the past. The now offers the choice and chance to start over, again and again and again. Living in the now creates endless opportunities to change your attitude and hence influence your daily reality.

I was born Lucille Jones in Harare, the capital of Zimbabwe, in the year 1971. My father was a musician who disappeared somewhere around my fourth birthday, never to be seen again. Dad's last name was Ilunga, but my mom, Julia Gaffley, decided that we were better off with the name Jones, as we were living in a country full of racism. Yep, that's right! She just chose an English name out of the blue and put it on our birth certificates! I can understand where she was coming from, considering the mood in Zimbabwe back then – apartheid was still holding Zimbabwe in its ugly claws when I came into this world.

I have one sibling, an amazing sister with whom I am fortunate enough to have a close, loving and supportive relationship. We had to work on it, as it was not always like this. My sister was the first person in my family to really understand my connection with meditation and self-realization. She is also the only other family member who has used meditation to transform herself and her life completely.

We became "soul sisters", not just blood sisters, sometime around our early thirties. Before that, we had lived on the same planet but in two different worlds, and we spoke two different languages. I spoke spiritual and my sister spoke material. She will probably laugh out loud when she reads this. One thing that all the women in our family are very good at is laughing. Some may not have lived very happy lives, but all of us are well known for our loud raucous laughter that does not need much to be released into the world.

My mom, a hard-working nurse and self-made entrepreneur, died when I was twenty-six years old. It is strange to think she was only one year older than I am now, forty-three, when pancreatic cancer took her from us. Mom had four sisters and one brother. My childhood was filled with aunts, as my uncle died in the War of Independence. One of my aunts also passed away when she was only a teenager from an infection in her leg that caused her to have a stroke. In my early childhood, my aunts would babysit us frequently and so we had disciplining coming at us from all directions.

Let me explain more about the spiritual-material comment regarding my sister. While I was searching for inner peace in India, meditating away for hours, my sister was working just as hard to gain financial freedom. You could even say she was a workaholic. We were both looking for freedom from the past that could lead us to a better future. I found that freedom in my spiritual pursuits and focus, and my sister found it through making money, something she has an incredible talent at doing.

During my extensive time in Asia, I would sometimes go home and stay with my sister, who has always been very loving and kind to me, even though we have had our fair share of huge fights and disagreements over the years. She never visited me while I was living in Asia, and I believe that this was mostly what caused us to grow apart. When we started living together in Switzerland, we had time to really rediscover each other.

Our childhood could be described as a tragicomedy, provided you have a good stomach for dark humor. At around the age of five, we were forced to live with my grandmother and her "draunkie" boyfriend, who had an insatiable thirst for alcohol. My grandmother was a dark, moody and foreboding character back in those days. She was always at the ready with a harsh word: a woman of little praise or affection. Strict rules in her household had to be followed to the letter or else you got a beating. Even peeing in bed, which is something kids grow out of naturally, was given close attention, and got you into serious trouble! You were forced to grow up fast or face the consequences. Her difficult relationship with the draunkie – a slang word well used in that neighborhood – may have been one reason for the smoke that seemed to constantly steam out of her ears. Back then there was at least one draunkie on every street in Sunningdale – a characteristic and sign of the times for the lower-class colored man. I remember one time when my sister and I came home from school. I was about eight years old. The draunkie was swaying wildly as he urinated on the floor in the corridor just outside the bedroom he shared with Gran! We giggled with disgust and horror, and we knew that night the shit was going to hit the fan when Gran got home. Shortly after that incident my grandmother threw him out, and I wish I could say she lived happily ever after. Let's just say, she lived.

My father, the musical egomaniac, seems to have vanished into thin air. He is said to have deserted my mother by disappearing sometime after I was born, although he reappeared again when I was four. Understandably, no one wanted to have anything to do with him at that point. Apparently not a single sign of life had come from him until the day he reappeared. Can you imagine how my mom must have felt having had two babies with this guy who just "up and left" after promising to be back within a few weeks and then was never to be heard from again for three years? She was barely an adult when she had us and began to endure this grueling situation. Each day that passed with no news must have just broken her heart. Days turned into weeks, weeks turned into months, and months turned into years. What we humans do to each other, especially to the people we claim to love, is shameful. Children need unconditional love from both parents. Parents should make sure that they do not allow their personal differences and problems to rob their children of having that priceless experience. Having said that, clearly this cannot always be avoided.

Shortly after my dad reappeared, he faced the full wrath of all the Gaffley women and very quickly disappeared again. This time, he was gone for good. Well, sort of gone. When I was about twelve, a letter appeared from him. It had a return address in Switzerland. I guess his path had led him there as a musician. Maybe he even played at the famous Montreux Jazz Festival. After we wrote back we never got a reply, so that was the end of that. Hope was lost again after history repeated itself and weeks became months and months became years with no contact! It was heartbreaking again. Since I serendipitously now live in Switzerland, I sometimes wonder when I see an older black man in the street: "Dad, is that you?" Yeah, I know, that's weird, right? I probably will never know what became of my father. My grandmother today still lives in the same house where I saw Dad for the last time all those years ago. All I remember about him is a very big fabulous Afro, light blue bell-bottom pants, high black platform boots and a yellow flower-printed shirt with a light blue waistcoat over it that matched the pants. Since I was only four then, I guess you could say I have always had a good eye for fashion and attention to detail. You could also say that my ability to be "the observer" got awakened within the drama of that last encounter with my father. From then on I've often had this way of being able to take in the world around me and see it and experience it in all its glorious splendor and intensity.

That last time we saw our father was pretty dramatic. He had been screaming that he wanted to see his children. My sister and I were locked in the back yard, where there was a chicken run, some fruit trees and a bountiful vegetable patch. We could see Dad through the gaps between the metal sheets that had been wired together to make a fence. My grandmother was holding a hosepipe and spraying my dad with it aggressively as he stubbornly attempted, in his ridiculous high boots and rather tight bell-bottoms, to climb over the locked front gate. Getting really angry about the water being blasted on to his face and Afro, Dad backed down and left, cursing and screaming all the way down the street. My sister and I, who somehow intuitively knew that something really significant was going on, cried hard in that deep silent way when no sound comes out but your mouth is frozen wide open and tears stream down your cheeks, the mouth closing only momentarily to wail painfully and suck in new oxygen to stop you from passing out. My grandmother's harsh treatment of our dad on that day was all too familiar and alarming to us. Yet after his abhorrent treatment of my mother and us, who can blame her?

We saw my mom as little as once a month while living with my stern Roman Catholic grandmother for a period of time which felt like a few lifetime sentences being served back to back in a maximum security prison. Mom's job in the hospital meant that she had to work a lot of night shifts, weekends and public holidays too. This living situation with my grandma went on for five years. The reasons given for this were money and our education. My mom could not afford daycare and a decent school that we "coloreds" were allowed to go to was in walking distance from my grandmother's place. Even the schools were still segregated back then.

The day finally came when we were to move back with Mom and her partner. My stepfather, Frank Langford, was an Englishman. He was more than thirty years my mom's senior. We were relieved when we found out that our days at Grandma's household were over. We were hardly able to sleep the night before we knew our mom was coming to pick us up. Our glee was short lived when it became obvious that Frank had wandering hands. Preying on us at every opportunity he could get, it started slowly and subtly over the years, but became increasingly unpleasant. This will probably come as a huge surprise to my family, or then again, maybe not! Who knows what deep dark secrets families are capable of hiding, for reasons that are mostly beyond comprehension? Revealing the truth can be more stressful and appears to cause more commotion than facing the horror of what actually happened, or worse, may even continue to happen.

My sister got the worst of it. My fiery nature which everyone said I always had may have saved me. However, every day I did have to deal with hands that wandered up my leg or alarmingly grabbed my bottom or brushed a boob. Once Frank stuck his disgusting old cigarette-tasting tongue down my throat right in the kitchen while we were doing the dishes together. My mom was in the next room watching *Dallas*! I was shocked to the core and almost threw up! Yet I said nothing, retreating deeper into myself. As much as I often wanted to blurt it out to my mom, I could not bring myself to tell. Her last boyfriend, Arthur, had also broken her heart badly. He was from Portugal. After living with Mom for some years, promising her the moon and the stars, he just disappeared back to Portugal without even so much as a phone call or letter. She did not look like she could take much more disappointment on that level! Without working with forgiveness, through the power of unconditional love, we are at risk of losing our sensitivity to what we really feel. A heart that has become hardened and tainted by heartbreak will most likely attract the wrong kind of love relationships into our lives. That is why keeping a "pure heart" is of the utmost importance. In upcoming chapters I will share with you precisely how to do this.

No one ever spoke to us about sexual abuse, so we were not prepared for it at all. Also, because it began slowly, over years, it was extremely confusing, and the fear of speaking out was great, especially since in our culture adults were always right. In most of Africa, this is the law of the land, no matter what your argument or concern may be. Children do not have a voice and are not protected from abuse or excess violence from adults. They are often made to feel a sense of being responsible for everything bad that happens to them. I dare not think about how often child abuse goes unpunished in Africa and even worse, unapologetically so.

Apparently my career as a rebel started at a young age. My aunts often talk about how, from the moment I could speak, I would fearlessly stand up to them, challenging their authority, my little eyes burning holes through their skulls as I stood tall in my white terry cotton nappy indignantly stomping my feet and making my imperial demands! Because of this attitude, I often saw a slipper, leather belt, peachy stick (deadly whiplike branch, picked fresh off a peachy tree, for the purpose of beating a child), dog collar with spikes, or big flat palm coming my way. My sister was the opposite of me, as the story is so often told. She was very lovely, quiet and much more obedient than I was. But even she did not escape the punishing blows of the harsh discipline. I remember one time I could hear the screaming and beating all the way down the street after some neighbor had claimed she had done something naughty.

One part of my childhood I do have very fond memories of is going to school. I loved it! I was good at it, and teachers loved me. I was definitely the teacher's pet in each grade. At school, feistiness was translated into "smart" and got a lot of acknowledgement. It was a place where I got to shine, get praise and receive affection. At the end of each year in junior high school, certificates were awarded to the top three students. I always received one of the certificates, much to the annoyance of my classmates. Even in high school that love affair continued. I really did adore my time at school and being away from the drama and rage, which seemed to be my home life. My school friends and I were all very tight. We spent as much time as was allowed playing hopscotch together, and we made up other games from old stockings or stones which we found in the garden. "Stonies" was one of my favorite games; you dug a small hole in the ground and filled it with little stones. Then you took another stone and threw that up into the air and had to pick a certain amount of stones out of the hole while the other stone was in the air. If you could catch the stone again, you progressed to the next amount or else it was someone else's turn to play. We had no computer games back then, so stonies would keep us busy for hours! With little money for toys, we were forced to be very creative, playing games with friends under the African sun, barefoot and a touch wild. At my grandmother's house I enjoyed connecting with nature. Loving the silence, I would often sit alone on the white bench under the shade of the big lemon tree in the front part of the garden, swinging my then-skinny legs playfully back and forth, absorbed in the smell of lemons while listening to the birds and the bees, the warm breeze gently kissing my cheeks. Staring out on to the colourful flower garden, deeply content to just rest there, suspended in a perfect moment.

Another aspect of my childhood that provides fond memories is the family gathering we had every Christmas. All the aunties, cousins, uncles, grandparents and so on would gather for a big party. These were decadent affairs, Zimbabwean style, of course! Everyone would bring their finest dishes, cakes and best behavior. The *braii* (barbecue grill) was piled up with nice cuts of beef and our favorite sausages. The mood was always high-spirited with funny stories being shared and received with loud laughter. My mom and her sisters were all very close and supportive of each other. We got presents from everyone. Even if the presents were mostly practical stuff like a new pair of school shoes or some underwear, it was still so much fun seeing them pile up! Plus, all the kids usually got a new pretty dress or suit for the occasion. The party feast always ended in dancing, something I have always loved and could have chosen as a career if life had not had other plans for me. Even as young as four, I would take my place and be in the center of the dance circle making everyone scream with delight at my Michael Jackson moves! Yes, these too were very good times.

Things at home with Frank got so bad for me that somewhere around my fourteenth birthday I tried to kill myself. I took a whole bottle of painkillers that the doctor had given me after a minor operation on my hand a few months before. The thing that I remember the most is getting home from the hospital, weak and dazed, and getting a call from my grandmother. She was yelling so loud I had to hold the phone away from my ear! "You stupid child! How could you do this to your mother! You selfish stupid child!!!!"

I remember wishing the suicide attempt had worked! She never even asked me why I did it or tried to understand the misery I may have been feeling to do such a thing. God forbid if the truth would be told. God forbid if you actually had feelings and an opinion that mattered.

My suicide attempt was never discussed with anyone in the family. If it did ever get mentioned, it was only to scold me and present me with further proof of my truly evil nature. I remember the feeling of longing to wake up from the nightmare that had become my daily reality. It was as if I were living a double life. In one life I was this carefree and joy-filled child who was fearless and at times dizzy with happiness. In those moments I was totally plugged into that natural freedom that children have direct access to. The kind of freedom that manifests as bellyache laughter and deep boundless love for the friends you play with every day. In my other life I felt alone, disconnected and trapped in the prison of my teenage mind. Thank goodness death had firmly rejected me! At some point peace did find me, and I learnt how to stay plugged into the childlike freedom and happiness that is beyond the snatching arms of the restless mind that tries to rob us of our "purity of heart".

I started modelling after a talent scout from a top agency saw me in a school play. I was dancing and lip-syncing in a lead role in *Cats*. Dancing was my greatest passion before I found meditation. I was trained in ballet till the age of twelve and then self-trained in modern dance. I used to watch the TV series *Fame* religiously, stealing moves and getting inspiration. Dance let me escape into a world where anything became possible and I felt like I could soar above it all.

Those afternoons I spent boldly daring to play my mom's precious records and dancing like a mad person for hours were my first conscious taste of this amazing inner ecstasy and peace. The movement brought me out of thinking and into the moment. Whatever sadness, fear and self-doubt I may have been feeling totally disappeared when I danced. I could lose myself in the music, the magic, the moment. I felt peace, I felt free and I felt happy to be alive. I felt connected. The world felt more beautiful and hopeful when I was dancing. Those long afternoon dance happenings were really my first taste of deep meditation, even if at the time I had no idea that that is what I was doing. I would lose track of time and become one with the world and the music as I closed my eyes and rolled my then-petite hips and twisted, twirled and whirled for hours, flying through the air, skillfully creating my own heady cocktail of ballet, modern jazz and hip-hop.

My grandfather was also a great dancer and even won some prizes in ballroom dancing. Being happy seemed to come naturally to him. I remember that he was often smiling, dancing and enjoying the moment. Even though he never had much wealth, you could see that he felt like a rich man. He was naturally connected to his inner joyful self, except (tragically) when he drank alcohol and Dr Jekyll became Mr. Hyde. Even though he came from the poorest family, one would never know it from his appearance. Most of his family still lived in mud huts and cooked on an open fireplace long after he had left their village and made for a better life for himself. Visiting them was always a trip for us suburban kids, especially the no electricity or running water part. The worst was the compost toilets! Grandpa was always elegantly dressed in a smart suit with black shoes that shone so bright you could see your reflection in them. He was an adventurer and extremely open minded, considering his conservative background. He left his home in Zimbabwe on foot and travelled to South Africa, where he met and fell madly in love my grandmother.

I remember taking my grandfather to the Reeperbahn (the famous red-light district in Hamburg) on one of his visits to Europe. His eyes nearly bulged out of his head. He had never seen anything like that in all his life. There is nothing like that in Zimbabwe. He could not stop laughing for days thereafter. He would burst into laughter as he recalled the transvestites that he had thought were women. I even took him to a peep show as part of his European educational tour! Zimbabweans are not into nudity. A lot of people do not even swim so never develop the habit of lying around in the sun wearing bathing suits. I must say that after one winter living in Europe, I was swiftly converted to a sun-worshiping maniac in a bikini!

At fourteen, I was earning my own money – big dollars compared to the average salary. I had dreams of making it big with my dancing and modelling. I did well in Zimbabwe, becoming somewhat of a supermodel there, doing a lot of different modelling gigs, some dance, TV commercials, newspaper advertisements and so forth on a weekly basis. I remember sometimes falling asleep in school because I had been up working on a weeknight. On the weekend, I normally had shows and more rehearsals.

I went to school till my O-levels. I would have loved to continue with further education, but had to leave early because my stepfather's sexual advances started to really get to me. By the time I left school, I was the first one in my family to pass the O-levels at the first attempt. It was an especially great achievement for someone who was always being called stupid or "dozy".

As staying at home was no longer an option, I had to start working full time and quit school when I was just seventeen years old. I moved into an all-girl hostel. I needed my mom's permission to live in the hostel because I was not yet eighteen. She refused to give it, which left me with no other choice than to tell her the truth about Frank. She signed the paper immediately, and the "whole thing" was never discussed again until some years later, when I brought it up again as part of my "letting go" process after my awakening. A heart tainted by pain, fear, disappointment and heartbreak may not act as you know it should and may even seem to have a nonsensical twisted will of its own. We have all possibly known this feeling to some lesser or larger degree. Why else would an otherwise perfectly reasonable, intelligent, loving woman continue to be with a man who has been sexually abusing her children for years?

I brought up the "whole thing" again because I wanted to know why it had never been discussed at the time when I was moving out from home. I also really wanted to understand why Mom had continued being with Frank even after she knew what he had done. That conversation was extremely uncomfortable for both of us, but also helped to bring us closer together. It gave me a chance for closure and to "walk my talk" and put forgiveness into practice. Forgiveness is an essential that we need to work with every single day if we are to be happy. Mother simply cried and could not look into my eyes. She apologized for not having the courage to do more, then and now. They continued together as a couple until the day the she died. Frank was never confronted and held accountable for his actions. Even Frank needs my forgiveness in order for me to be happy in the now. Living peacefully in the now demands the best of us, uncompromisingly! Forgiveness comes through understanding love. Love is what we become when we are willing to go beyond the limits of our ego. How did I forgive Frank? Through understanding that we need to extend forgiveness and compassion to all beings (without exception) if we seek freedom from personal suffering.

Forgiveness is the willingness to surrender our blame, anger and resentment, to become the embodiment of love. This means holding no ill will to even our worst enemies. This means "letting go" through the practice of forgiveness. All humans, good and bad, are a result of the collective consciousness to which we all contribute. That is why individual transformation is so key to bringing about the change we want to see in the world.

The hostel was a refreshing, exciting place and it was there I experienced my first taste of adulthood and freedom! I continued to model and dance in my spare time, but I also worked full time in a shop selling high-fashion clothing to rich businesspeople. Then I received a sudden welcomed promotion – I was asked to help with putting collections together for the shop. The store manager realized that I had a natural flair for fashion, combined with a sharp eye for detail. I helped choose the fabrics and even sketched some ideas, which were included in the new collections.

Even without formal training, I have ability in all things creative, such as painting, interior decorating, cooking and so forth. I also especially love "making over" my friends and even people I work with – if they will allow me to! Most people do not realize how gorgeous they are and dress to reflect this lack of confidence. I love seeing their faces when they realize what they have been hiding from themselves and others!

I also enjoy writing and I have even written, sang on and produced my own music CD, *Pearls of Wisdom, the Secrets of an Open Heart*. It is definitely a kind of music diary expressing feelings that needed to find a way out of me! My sister is, among other things, a very talented singer and songwriter who inspired me to give it a go as well. We love music – it seems to flow through our veins. It might be something we inherited from our dad.

Creativity is food for my soul. I need to express myself creatively to flourish in this life. It is important to find what feeds your soul with positive light. If you are to be happy, it is an essential. When I turned eighteen, another stroke of good fortune led me to a great opportunity. The lady who ran the model agency I was working for decided to quit from one day to the next. She jumped on a plane to America to follow her own dreams, leaving the owner in a big panic – and was never heard from again. The boutique and the modelling agency where I worked had the same owner, so when I heard what was going on I volunteered to "hold down the fort" at the agency until a solution was found. That's how I got the job running Zollies Modelling Agency, one of the top modelling agencies in Zimbabwe at that time. A few weeks later they also hired a wonderful lady named Gae. We made a dynamic team. I was living my passion. I was young and healthy. I loved what I was doing and I was making good money. For a brief window of time I was ecstatic – my life was good. Everything was going perfectly. Then I got married!

Love

I had already had my heart smashed to bits at fourteen when my first boyfriend, Kevin, had sex with one of my best friends. Come to think about it, that was a double whammy. Ouch! I had been on a mission to stay a virgin till I was eighteen. So the most we ever did was kiss fully clothed and "No wandering hands, please! Thank you!" I was surprised to learn that girls my age were daring to have sex at all. Coming from a woman-rich family, we never heard the end of how awful our lives would become if we were dozy enough to have sex and fall pregnant. Abortion was completely illegal in Zimbabwe, and teenage pregnancy was rampant and definitely a sin that would leave you burning in hell for all eternity. I was terrified enough by that thought to do everything in my power to avoid that fate.

Does Christianity realize how terrifying the idea of hell is to a child? I know I was frightened of God's wrath for a very long time! I was so scared of the devil coming to get me that if I was alone, I could not sleep with the light off until I was twenty-four. That changed after a few weeks in Lucknow with my teacher Papaji (whom you will soon meet). I just got out of bed one night and to my own surprise switched off the light. And that was the end of that trip! The fear was gone. Papaji showed me that there was nothing to be afraid of because dualities like good and evil exist only in the mind. When you can go beyond the mind, you see that there is only one source from which everything rises and goes back to. This source when you experience it directly is the most warm, enveloping and consuming positive energy you will ever know. It's like being safe and warm in your mommy's belly. This energy feeds your soul and you grow. Fear melts like falling snow on a warm spring day in the presence of that energy. That energy lies, awake or sleeping, within every human heart.

Now, I don't believe in the devil any more than I believe in hell. Our free will can create hell on earth for people around us and for ourselves. The only thing that will stop you from doing bad things is your conscience. The price you could pay for your so-called "sins" is your own sanity – as is evident in people who do very bad things to other people. They appear to end up mentally disturbed on some level. Most of them live without regret or even the awareness that what they did was wrong. That's how things like the Holocaust, slavery and apartheid can happen. The lack of compassion and consideration for other people's feelings seems to eat away our good nature, leaving nothing but an empty cave where our humanity used to be. Why, if "He" could, does "God" not stop them? Could it be because the truth of the matter is that only the people who do bad things could have stopped themselves, can stop themselves; by somehow finding their way back to the peace-loving heart? By finding their way back to a real compassion and respect for other human beings.

Neville, my first long-term boyfriend, had quit school and was doing an apprenticeship in toolmaking. He was tall and muscular in a way that made my teenage hormones go crazy. He always had black grease under his fingernails, but also had more charm than was legal. I remember how after only our first meeting he had the balls to knock on our door. Meeting my parents for the first time, he somehow managed to convince my mom and Frank the paedophile – who, ironically, was a police officer – that they should let him take us (my sister and me) out to a braai. I don't know how he did it, but sure enough, we were set free to mingle with people our own age at a party, chomping on succulent steaks and sipping Fanta. I was fifteen, and this date was heaven on earth! Until then, we had not even been allowed to go to a school disco, which was something we resented our parents for – depriving us the joy of "shaking it" to hot beats with our school friends. These discos were reported to be epic events that were talked about for months, before and after. Unfortunately for us, discos were apparently the devil's favorite pickup joints for recruiting young minds to join his team!

Neville even managed to convince my parents and his parents that I should spend most weekends at his place. We were strictly not allowed to see each other during the week. That was the only rule that did not melt in the face of Neville's charms. He lived in the garage at his parents' house. Even though the deal was that I would sleep in the main house and share a room with his sister Charmaine, he of course would sneak me into his room when he was sure everybody in the house was out cold. We giggled, talked and tossed around most of the night, and at dawn I would sneak back into my bed. I know it's a freaking miracle that we never did have sex, but it's true. I don't know how I managed to get any schoolwork done on those weekends, but my grades never slipped. We dated for three years, from fifteen till eighteen and against all the odds and the mean family bets that I would crash and burn and end up knocked up. I did stick to the virgin-till-eighteen plan. I think you know how I spent the night of my eighteenth birthday!

Then along came Chris, my first husband, and my life totally turned upside down. I had developed into a happier person by the time we met. Leaving home, having a great job at the modelling agency and having a cool boyfriend who adored me and could make me laugh had all done wonders for my self-confidence. I was in a really good place.

Chris was Swiss. We met in a devil's lair in Harare. The chic Archipelago nightclub was a playground for people of all colors, nationalities and age groups. He walked up to me, working his way through the crowd, his eyes never leaving mine. Without introducing himself, he asked in a very concerned voice, "Are you feeling sick?" "Why are you asking?" I replied, looking alarmed and adjusting my big late-eighties hair self-consciously while doing a quick count in my head of vodka oranges consumed. I had noticed him staring at me for some time already.

"Because", he said, laughing openly at me, "you have not danced for five minutes now". It was corny, but it made me smile. He was right! I had been out there for at least three hours straight! A normal scene was me smashing up the Archipelago dance floor, totally lost in the bass!

We dated for two years before we got married. I celebrated my twenty-first birthday the same year that we married, and by twenty-two I was signing the divorce papers. Chris was ten years older than me. The whole thing never stood a chance. He wooed me out of Neville's arms and charms with giant boxes of mouth-watering Swiss chocolate, gigantic bouquets of flowers, expensive perfume, several fancy restaurants and several buckets of champagne – things I had never indulged in before Chris turned me on to them. During the time B.C. (Before Chris), I had lived a simple life, saving all the money I could so I could escape from Zimbabwe. There really was not much indulging in anything. Chris was a good guy, but not without his own set of problems. There had been drama in his childhood too, but I won't go into the details. He was successful, tall, dark and good looking (when I kept him away from his beloved Coke and Swiss chocolates). He had an insatiable appetite for both; then add to that his favorite meal of pasta with butter. Chris had his heart in the right place and a wicked sense of humor, but he took it too far sometimes with the funny guy routine. Engraving "To My Beloved PITA" in my wedding ring was one of those times. "Pita" was the nickname he used to call me and it translates directly into "Pain in the ass!" With that in my wedding ring, the marriage was surely doomed.

During the stormy, eye-opening relationship with Chris, I learnt my first really big and fundamental life lesson: "Money can't buy you happiness or peace of mind, but it sure can buy you nice shoes and handbags!" An excellent lesson to get out of the way while you are still young, don't you think? We all know that feeling of being convinced that if we could just get more money, get our debts paid, buy that dream car, send our kids to the best schools, happiness and peace of mind will surely finally be ours. There is no denying the comforts money can buy, but you can be sure happiness is not one of them. The source of happiness is within and not without. Many who have acquired all they ever dreamed of will vouch for this.

During the time A. C. (After Chris), I again started to realize just what a mess I was emotionally. Having been brought up a Roman Catholic meant praying every day before each meal and at bedtime as well as attending church every Sunday. These visits included embarrassing private face-to-face confessions with the white local priest, Father Thomas. There was no screen, just the priest's pale, stern face staring down at you from his special chair. Him in his special robes as you knelt humbly at his special feet feeling especially ashamed to have even have been born!

My religion, besides frightening me, also filled me with self-doubt and shame and offered no peace of mind whatsoever. Growing up with both parents away, it didn't seem to me God was doing a good job looking after me or answering my prayers. I was angry with him but too scared to admit it to anyone! I could only imagine the look on Father Thomas's face if I had blurted out, "Now let me tell you what I really think of your God! He is terrifying and he doesn't seem to care much about anything!" Even priests back then were allowed to beat you if they thought that would put some sense back into you! I always saw much hypocrisy from those who preached God's words the loudest. The whole thing was so confusing.

I was only twenty-one at the time we married. I had too much baggage and Chris did too. Our relationship had lasted three and a half years. Chris's financial generosity along with the Swiss nationality I gained when we married gave me a new level of freedom when we parted ways. Zimbabweans are basically prisoners in their country unless they are super rich. Then they can buy their way out of and into most countries. With a Zimbabwe passport you cannot travel anywhere without a visa and an invitation letter from a host. No host – no visa. Unless, that is, you can show large funds just sitting in your bank account. Having the possibility to move around the world freely has been such an enormous blessing in my life. I always say my life is turning out better than I could ever have planned it!

Love, happiness and peace were states I wanted so much back then while dating and in my marriage to Chris. But like most people, I had no clue how to achieve them. By the time I was twenty-three I felt like a hundred. Anyone who has ever got divorced will know what I mean. It is a grueling process. I was tired of crying, hurting, fighting, feeling hopeless and hating myself for not being lovable, but having no idea how to stop feeling that way!

If you don't know who you are and how to be happy with yourself, regardless of what is happening around you, even great abundance will not bring you peace of mind. Chris and I had it all and we should have been elated, but we just argued a lot and both earned our master's degrees in how to make each other miserable. We lived in a beautiful house that had a stunning garden, a swimming pool and even an outdoor Jacuzzi. We had help around the house, a gardener and a maid that took care of our every whim. I had a glamorous career. We travelled extensively to Paris, London, New York and so on. "The world was my oyster". If only I had known how to enjoy oysters!

Now don't think I didn't enjoy myself. Of course we also had some wonderful, fun and passionate times together. I have some magnificent memories of those fairy-tale adventures we had. Being with Chris made me feel like a princess. But ultimately our lack of personal happiness as individuals made living together in harmony impossible. There was much blaming and pointing fingers and very little owning and taking responsibility.

The truth, as much as we might continue to ignore it, is that this happiness I speak of has nothing to do with how much we have or don't have at any given moment. We stubbornly hang on to the idea that having things will be the answer to our problems. When your peace of mind or inner joy "in-the-now" depends on material success, you will never be truly content. Because of our desires we always want more. When you get what you want, you again want something else and this cycle will continue endlessly – unless you stop it and allow yourself to fully enjoy and appreciate the moment as it is right now.

When Chris and I divorced, I decided I needed to get out of Zimbabwe for a fresh start. The country felt too small for the two of us. After a number of complex and crazy events and amazing serendipities which included a decision to pursue my passion for cooking, meeting the beautiful Princess Diana, a brief rock-and-roll stopover in Milan and a disturbing encounter with an Italian god, I found myself somewhere I never thought I would ever end up in a million billion years! In India, in an ashram, dressed in a long flowing white robe meditating on a cold marble floor. Before I experienced this ashram in Pune, I never even knew or could imagine such a wonderful place existed in the world. India was spellbinding and intoxicating: the colors, the smell of the air, the chaos. The saris, gold, beggars, yogis, poverty, rickshaws, singing, dancing, worshipping, malas, monsoon rain, unbearably hot summers, unbelievable markets and deliriously delightful food variations. Everywhere you looked or went, your senses were slapped awake. I felt like I had landed on a different planet! I seemed to be making love to the world around me. India was orgasmic in its stunning, intense beauty and macabre indifference to your sensibilities. I very quickly fell in love with her and what she awoke in me.

The ashram felt to me like an oasis in the desert. It was a fresh place, full of exotic plants, flowers and people. Even the air in there seemed to be filled with something extra: electricity, peace and hope. I was clueless when I arrived. Despite my fog of complete skepticism, I still was very touched just being by there. If you can, imagine the perfect combination of innocence and naiveté swirling around me as I walked through that ashram on that first day – twenty-three going on to thirteen going on to thirty!

I can see now that my spiritual journey started way before I was even aware of being on a journey. Everything that happened to me had beautifully prepared me for what happened next. Every experience was placed perfectly on the path of my life, so I was ready to hear the truth and be set free. I would like to share with you the three people in my life that have greatly contributed to all that I am now. Through meeting them I have prospered, through their love I have learnt and for their guidance I remain eternally grateful.

Osho

Osho is a controversial Indian guru who has left some people divided in their opinion of him and what happened in his communities. As previously mentioned, my focus has always been on my own spiritual growth and not on him or the crowd around him. I personally like him and I am glad he and his teachings came into my life. I cannot say I agree with all the choices he made, but I do think he was ahead of his time and an out-of-the-box thinker!

He was a highly provocative and extremely intelligent man. He had already left his body when I arrived at his ashram sometime in 1993. It was there when I sat on the white marble floor of his beautiful Buddha Hall that my inner eyes fluttered open. It happened during my first-ever meditation at the first evening group session. An old video of one of Osho's discourses was being shown as was done every night at a celebration called the White Robe Brotherhood. Which sounds more sinister than it was! Everyone had to wear a beautiful white robe to the meeting.

Osho, projected on to a huge screen, spoke very slowly, as if he was caressing your soul with his words. I remember being very amused at first, thinking "Give me whatever he's having!" He looked so peaceful and content. His voice, one of his greatest assets, was clear, eloquent and filled with a great passion and conviction that came from somewhere very deep. I had honestly never heard anyone speak from such a powerful place.

What he was saying was not new to me. It was stuff I had always known. I just never had the chance to meet someone whose focus was on happiness rather than sadness. On positivity rather than negativity and on gratitude rather than lacking. It was refreshing and extremely uplifting and engaging. Until that day, I had no clue about meditation or meditating. I had never read a spiritual book in my life except parts of the Bible. I had come to this place through the recommendation of the sexy Italian god I mentioned earlier. Claudio had visited Osho Ashram many times while Osho was still alive, and when he saw the look of sad despair in my eyes, I guess he thought I desperately needed something this place had to offer.

Claudio never explained much to me about what to expect other than describing it as one of the most beautiful places he had ever been in the whole world. I was intrigued and ready for some kind of adventure when he suggested I drop my plan of flying to Miami and hop on a plane to India instead. Without much thought, I said "Yes!" and bought myself a one-way ticket to Bombay. Twenty-four hours later I landed in India, alone. After spending a very strange night in Bombay, which included a 3 a.m. kiss from a rat in a dive hotel (I kid you not!), I took a two-hour taxi ride to Pune in the front seat of a cab that was going at breakneck speeds, hooting loudly and wildly all the way.

So there I was, gazing up at Osho on a big screen, listening with great concentration and focus to every word he was saying. He had a quirky, long salt-and-pepper beard and he wore a long, ornately embellished blue silk robe and the most massive diamond-studded watch I have ever seen. The energy around me was too peaceful for me to feel afraid, even though I was way out of my comfort zone. I had no idea at that point that my life was about to change completely. Something unimaginably great was about to happen to me, right there on my first day at Osho Ashram.

His words started to burn a hole through my closed mind and his simple powerful wisdom penetrated thick layers of my skepticism. I started to relax. I took a deep breath and decided that I liked this Osho guy and could understand why he commanded such great respect from the hundreds around me. The moment of my transformation started with a small smile on my face that turned into an intense feeling of happiness. His words were stirring deep emotions in me. "This moment is all we truly have" – long pause. "Make every moment a celebration!" – longer pause. "Once celebration penetrates your being, it continues. Then there is no holiday needed, the whole of life becomes a celebration". He too a deep breath and with one of his bushy eyebrows raised elegantly he said, "Let go of the past sadness and the future worries. Wake up to all the beauty that is around you, right here and now the world is full of beauty, you are full of beauty. Life is here now and mind is never here now, go beyond the mind!"

As his soothing, hypnotic voice exploded gently into the silence, his fiery gaze bore into me from the big screen. His unfading presence hung in the thick silence that surrounded his words, weaving back together the pieces of my broken heart with an invisible delicate thread of pure compassion. That's when my focus totally shifted and I experienced being fully present and relaxed in the now. That's the moment in my life when I started to live and stopped waiting to die. One minute I was this sad, tired and lonely woman with so many things going through my mind and even more emotions weighing me down! The next minute I was peace itself and it felt like the world and all its problems had just vanished around me. The feeling descended upon my being like a warm, powerful avalanche. It destroyed everything in its pathway. Only a deep silence remained where my spinning mind had been. Where my negative emotions had lived, rampantly fornicating and multiplying, was only a sweet pulsing tenderness and softness. It was a feeling so fine, like that which one gets when looking across the calmest, smoothest surface of a lake upon which the sun dances passionately yet with the utmost delicacy. I felt clearer and calmer than I could ever remember feeling. This experience changed me then in ways that only became obvious in the weeks that unfolded afterwards. I was never the same after that night.

The silence in my head was so deep it felt loud. Someone had pressed the pause button. Sadness and fears that had been unconsciously holding me down melted away from my mind and body like chocolate on the tongue – slowly, sweetly – and simply delightful. A fountain of good feelings was opened up inside and bubbled through all my senses. I stopped feeling sorry for myself as suddenly as a hard rain sometimes abruptly ends.

Tears rolled down my cheeks because the experience was so exquisite. I did not want to open my eyes or move in case I might interrupt the process. I just sat there, still and content, long after the Osho video had come to an end and the last of the hundreds that were gathered there that night had left. When I finally moved, I stood up on shaky legs that had gone to sleep. I felt transformed, empowered and still very much connected to these new and wonderful feelings of deep peace and intense happiness. Being on my own and having just arrived that day, I had no one to tell about what I had just experienced and what I was still experiencing, so I just returned to my hotel room and fell into bed with a happy sigh. I felt drunk with these new joyful feelings and was asleep in minutes.

I slept very deeply that night and when I woke up I was still smiling. I remember that because of how odd it felt. It was the first time in my life that I had noticed waking up with a smile. Thank goodness it was not the last time. As soon as I had my breakfast at the German Bakery, a well-known spot for Osho *sannyasins*, I returned to my hotel room and sat to meditate. I still had no clue what meditation really was or how to do it, but I just knew I wanted to stay connected to this newfound peace of mind that this place and the amazing Osho had revealed to me.

During that first solo flight into myself I ended up sitting for hours. I was shocked when I looked at my watch afterwards. Two hours had passed! I repeated the same thing at sunset that evening, gazing in wonder into my newfound inner world. This routine went on for the next seven years. Every single day I would meditate for a minimum of four hours a day. It was effortless for me to meditate – I absolutely loved it. It felt like something I was born to do!

I would sit silently, just observing my thoughts. I would see where they came from and where they disappeared to. I quickly realized that through this observation of my thoughts and my focus on the silence in between them, the silence would start to grow and grow until there were no thoughts at all. Just long stretches of silence broken only by some random images. Since negative thinking had caused so much stress during my life, especially the months before, during and after my divorce, this ability to be peaceful and thought-free was so refreshing and liberating. I reveled in it. I realized that I would never have to be a victim of my negative thoughts and feelings if I could just master the art of being. Through meditation one can learn how to connect to inner peace, regardless of what is going on in one's life at any given moment.

This newfound peace was my secret. I never spoke about my experiences to anyone. I noticed many people in the ashram struggling with themselves. They were doing a lot of workshops and group sessions to help them experience a breakthrough. I instinctively knew I had to protect my wonderful experience from other people's sceptical and judgmental minds. We humans can so easily shift into that mode when something happens which we can't quite understand or even accept.

So in the next six months that I was at the ashram, I went quietly about my business. I learnt a lot more about spirituality, energy, love, sex, meditation, truth and freedom within those months than I had in my entire life up till that point. I saw every moment as an opportunity to put being happy and content in the now into practice. With so much opportunity to practice, you cannot fail. I loved sitting silently connecting to the energy of contentment and deep peace that would fill me up. I was like a kid in a candy store. I just couldn't get enough of this taste of freedom.

I moved to Lucknow to meet Papaji after six months of fully absorbing Osho's teaching's and enjoying the incredible depth, creativity, vitality and diversity of his amazing ashram. Those months were full of wild, weird and wonderful stories. Let's just say my passion for living started there, because I woke up to the moment. This awakening got me in touch with some powerful energies and new ways of experiencing the world. This attracted some interesting and way-out-there characters to me, with whom I shared some pretty mind-blowing and mind-boggling experiences. This was good because it allowed me to see the infinite possibilities such an awakening can offer and let me choose my own way on this path at the early stages. The experiences I had with some of these amazing people made me realize some important stuff that kept me firmly on the right way. The right way for me.

I realized I was not into talking to angels or saints or dead people. I prefer a direct conversation with my own heart. I was also not into developing shamanic powers that could make rain fall from the sky at my command. I know that sounds like fun, but I quickly saw that it could also be highly dangerous energy work. Especially when you have the wrong teacher. The guy who tried to teach me this unfortunately turned out to be a very dark character. I was not into fortune telling either. I prefer not knowing what might happen next and just going with the flow. Creating and changing my reality as I go, developing my own intuitive skills to predict the outcome of my actions. I was not into having odd out-of-body experiences like taking over the body of a bird and then flying through the sky. I met people who claimed they could do that. And I definitely was not going to get on an alien spaceship with someone who believed that they were half alien and half human. The line between fiction and reality blurred at times as I attracted and met every kind of seeker of knowledge you can think of. My journey weaved in and out between the surreal and the sublime! Now don't get me wrong. I was open enough to have some very unusual and wonderful experiences with all these things. That's how I know I am not into them! And I promise to share more details of these stories one day.

"Each one to his own, when it harms no one". I have nothing against people who seek these experiences, but I know that ultimately it may distract from what one was looking for in the first place: just good old-fashioned inner peace in the here and now. These encounters made me realize that this was really all that I was after.

Through self-realization, gifts come to one naturally: a powerful voice of wisdom from within, a sharpened intuition and ability to know things, a mental clarity, a deep realization that you are not your physical body. It gives one freedom and allows one to be more flexible, easygoing and open. I also started to notice small things I had never paid attention to before, such as the constantly changing smell of the air, the shifting dance of light, the intensity of colors. I was more alive. It is like living in a slow-motion, timeless now instead of being in fast-forward or rewind.

As great as it was at Osho Ashram, I knew I had grown wings and it was time to soar to even higher levels of self-development. I knew that I needed a living teacher to show me how to do that, to take the next step – or another quantum leap! I could see how Osho's teachings were misunderstood or reinterpreted by some of his disciples to suit the "we are followers rather than leaders" mindset. They believed no one could ever be as great as him because he was a genius. He had a photographic memory that gave him access to all the knowledge he had ever soaked up from books, combined with his astonishing power to fill people with light. He most certainly was awe-inspiring. Yet still I could not help feeling that they had lost sight of the fact that he was just a mirror and a human being like themselves. It was time for me to step out of the familiar and comforting Osho nest to seek answers to the questions I still had about self-realization.

My Personal Journey into Freedom

I knew I could never go back to the superficial world of modelling. I feel strongly against what the modelling culture does to a woman's self-confidence. Not only the woman modelling, but all women. Imagine me, this model with dreams of becoming a great chef! I loved eating, but modelling added to eating for me equaled being miserable every second of the day because every bite I took was filled with dread and guilt. Modelling is far less glamorous when you go behind the scenes, and these days it may even be worse, with girls even being too old at twenty! The modelling industry uses teenage girls and boys to torture us and make us feel bad about how we look. Why are we still allowing this to happen? What effect are these images having on the confidence of our young girls and boys? Size zero is what it has all come down to! Yet we remain loyal to the magazines that parade these extremes, keeping them in business!

Interesting story – in the early 90s I was in L.A. in the hip and happening Spargo restaurant, at least it was hip and happening back then. I was using the ladies' room when from my booth I heard a woman almost crying with displeasure about how fat she looked and how unhappy she was about it. Can you imagine my shock and horror when I came out to see a stunningly beautiful Claudia Schiffer eyeing herself in the mirror with distaste and almost looking like she was about to burst into tears? At that time Ms. Schiffer was on every news and magazine stand, her gorgeous face and body tormenting women all over the world. She was the supermodel who crossed borders with her success. From Tokyo to L.A. people knew her name and that killer body was worshiped! She looked absolutely, unbelievably luscious and stunningly beautiful. Hell, given the chance even I would do her! My eyes could hardly believe what they were seeing and my ears were crying out for her to stop talking nonsense!

I knew after that day that I would have to find something else to do, something else that I was good at. If Claudia was so concerned with her body, what chance did I ever stand to be happy in such an industry? And let me tell you something: I've got some serious African butt that made Claudia's look like somebody needed to give her an extra-large double fudge chocolate chip cookie!

Through watching trained professional dancers in the ashram, I also discovered that I would not be able to compete in Europe or America with that standard of dancer, as I was only self-trained in modern dance and already twenty-three years old. It felt like the old me, Lucille, was morphing into someone new, gaining some good habits while losing some bad ones. By gaining new dreams, my life gained new priorities, focus and direction.

Shortly before I decided to leave Pune, I decided I was finally ready to participate in the big ceremony at the ashram, where one was given a new name. I decided I would use the new name only if I liked it more than the name I already had. I received the name Prem Mahima, which was said to mean "majesty of love". Using the new name was a no-brainer! I dropped the Prem – that made the whole thing too long-winded – and became Mahima to all the people I met from that day on. It was such a convincing transformation that every member of my family now calls me Mahima, except once in a while when "Lucy" just slips out against their will or as a test of my patience. I wonder what they would say if they knew they were calling me "majesty"!

Role of the teacher

As guidance is an important aspect of individual self-development, I would like to highlight some important things to consider when seeking guidance from a teacher, coach, preacher, guru or any other authority figure you may be working with.

What is the role of the teacher on a journey to rediscover your inner peace and integrity? It is an important part of learning and growing quickly, and that's why the following is so relevant.

It is important to find someone who "walks their talk" and speaks from the heart, not the mind. I have had a few amazing hearts guiding me. What is important is not to fall into the group mentality. There will always be a crowd around teachers that want you to think or act as they do.

You don't want the crowd to decide your fate, to dictate who you are and what you can or cannot achieve. In most groups around a teacher (leader), you will mostly find that the surrounding crowd believes that their leader, guru, teacher, priest, rabbi, doctor or whoever is at the top of the pyramid. Then there is a sizable gap, and then comes the rest of us. If you buy into this belief you will follow blindly, switching off your ability to trust and empower yourself. Look deeper into religious groups or ashrams with powerful teachers and leaders, and you will find this belief festering in its core, disempowering the masses that follow. Keep your focus on the teacher and his teachings and not the group.

Use the teacher to grow. Surrender your ego and learn all you can. But do not buy into the idea that the teacher is better than you. This will dramatically block your ability to grow. It may be true that a teacher has discovered some things that you may not yet know how to fully access, but that does not make him or her better than you, only different. Teachers who are too keen on focusing on how little you know compared to them should set your alarm bells ringing. Be warned – people can be different from us without being put high up on a pedestal (or the reverse, us treating them as lower-class citizens).

You would be wise to remember that teachers, regardless of how great and wise they may appear to be, are also human. Even with their great wisdom, they can make mistakes, lose their cool or be imperfect. Being aware and awake does not make you less human. Looking for perfection in human beings is a pointless waste of precious time. Find someone you feel comfortable with, someone you can open up to and who you believe is truly speaking from that deep heart which makes you feel moved even through your scepticism. Don't be too quick to run away when you spend more time with them and discover, "Oh, they are only human too!"

Knowing this will help you to also become more tolerant and patient with yourself. I say all this because I have seen so many seekers of peace get lost in glorifying their teachers, seeming to have forgotten the reason they came to them in the first place. They lose themselves in the apparent amazingness of the teacher instead of learning from them.

Keep your focus on yourself! Get lost in your own heart, your own amazingness. This will help you truly find yourself and not lose yourself in the teacher. Respect them, even admire them, but don't glorify them and create a belief that they have reached a level you could never reach. Only you can put a limit on your own potential and what is possible. There is a reason why teachers of great integrity will say, "There is no difference between us!" Believe them. Don't compare yourself or your life to that of your teacher, priest, role model or guru. Who knows how enlightened you would feel if you had people around you every day totally adoring you, listening closely to your every word, taking care of your every wish and all with the greatest of devotion, respect and love! I am guessing you would feel fanfreakingtastic!

Who knows how they would cope walking in your shoes – standing in the queue at the supermarket on a busy Saturday afternoon, dealing with rush hour traffic after a long day at work, or waking up at the crack of dawn to feed hungry children before rushing off to spend all day in an office.

Who knows? They may not find it so fanfreakingtastic! So keep your focus on learning how you can get the confidence and self-belief they have. It is what has contributed to their ability to manifest the life they have. Figure out what gives them such incredible conviction and clarity, because they are living their dream!

Learn, but don't envy or worship and make yourself small. Use the knowledge of the teacher to empower yourself and enrich and transform yourself and your life. It is impossible for your life to stay the same when you start to really connect to yourself. Things that do not belong to your true being will fall away from you and your life. This may include job changes, clarification of relationships, maybe even moving to a new country or city. Miracles have happened and are always happening in my own life due to my commitment to loving silence.

Teachers are all just mirrors reflecting you to yourself. Whatever greatness you see in them, immense beauty and strength, it's all in you too. Own it, embrace it, and awaken to your own inner strength and wisdom. You are making important decisions every day that will shape your life according to where your focus is. Start changing your focus if you want to see change in your life. The three important steps I will give you to focus on will bring more peace, love and happiness into you in the now.

Stay an individual, think for yourself and become your own master. You are way more naturally intelligent spiritually than you give yourself credit for. That's why most of what you will read, you already know on some level. This will just be a reminder to give you an extra boost and push you deeper out of superficiality and into your natural spirituality.

This book is not about developing praying-to-a-higher-power skills. You don't even have to believe in God to personally benefit, because it is all about connecting to more integrity, compassion, love, kindness and generosity in you, which is something we all can work on, whatever our religious beliefs or spiritual orientation may be.

Papaji

When I – Mahima/Majesty – arrived in Lucknow, nothing could have prepared me for what was going on there. I entered through a small side gate into a big, but plain, old house in the middle of a suburban neighborhood called Indira Nagar. A round-faced, fiercely happy-looking older gentleman sat on a very fancy chair which was magnificently decorated with hundreds of fresh flowers. He was surrounded by about a hundred people sitting at his feet. His head was swaying gently to the lively music being played by his students. He looked very regal in a dazzlingly white kurta. Orange flower garlands were draped playfully around his neck. His bald head was so shiny that you could imagine it had been polished.

You could see that there were people from all over the world gathered there in that room. Some had their eyes closed, looking totally happy and filled with joy. Some were staring up at Papaji as if he had just descended directly from the clouds. Others were singing passionately and rocking back and forth. A few were up on to their feet, heads thrown back, with their arms waving gently through the air, tears of joy streaming down some faces. The air was electric – full of energy, power and great enthusiasm! I stood at the side, staring hard, trying not to judge, but failing miserably! The scepticism I had lost that first night with Osho had crept back into my mind. I was wondering how, if at all, I was going to fit into this new and very interesting setup. The session was just ending on that first day I arrived. So I did not have a chance to meditate and see if anything was different being around this teacher – who was still in his body.

I was to discover later that evening that being around Papaji would definitely open new doors of experience. As he was leaving the relatively tiny hall (compared to Osho's great enormous Buddha Hall), he stopped in front of me. I realized he was a very tall man with an even taller presence. He asked me which country I was from. I gave him my hand and introduced myself, answering his question. In that moment, the crowd around him burst into laughter. He looked amused too but politely and gently shook my hand. This evoked more ripples of laughter from his attentive audience, who seemed to react to every move he made. As we gazed into each other's eyes intensely – in those brief seconds – I decided that this Papaji guy had his heart in the right place.

He moved on and stopped to speak to other people in the crowd. The audience moved too, like his shadow! Bodies pressed tightly to get closer to him, and that's when I noticed people diving to his feet and kissing them passionately. I understood why people had laughed at my handshake greeting. It was not the protocol around here. I remember sniggering to myself, "That would never be me!" Groveling at someone's feet like that seemed weird, undignified and unnecessary. Needless to say, within a few weeks of my arrival there, yes, I too was throwing myself wholeheartedly to the ground. I too was kissing those rough corned feet – which had seen eighty-odd years of living – with as much gusto and enthusiasm as if they were tender baby's feet!

During our brief encounter that first afternoon Papaji invited me to have dinner at his house that same evening. I had a powerful, unusual and somewhat alarming experience in his living room. He was still getting ready for dinner when I arrived, so I sat with some other guests meditating on a cushion. After about five minutes of sitting there, I entered into a totally new experience – even to this day I cannot find the words to describe exactly what happened. I will, however, give it my best shot: I could no longer move my body. It felt like I had lost gravity and was falling, falling, falling!

My crown chakra was fully activated. For those who are unfamiliar with chakras, it is the one on top, directly in the middle of the head.

It felt like there was an energy cylinder coming from the sky through the top of my head and into the ground. Tears started rolling down my face just at the moment Papaji entered the room. Everyone rose to their feet to greet him respectfully, except for me, as I was firmly glued to the floor. I could not even open my eyes. I could feel Papaji's eyes burning into me! He asked what was wrong with me in a concerned voice. I could not speak. I just sat there with a mini-waterfall running down my cheeks, even though I did not feel like I was crying. My body and face were still and I did not feel any particular emotion. The experience was not unpleasant, but at the same time it was very strange because my body would not do what I wanted it to do. I could hear the people around me talking, but I could not respond. I could hear Papaji asking a lot of questions about me, trying to understand what was happening to me. He asked his personal doctor to examine me. She was on duty all the time and was part of Papaji's inner circle. She found nothing physically wrong with me through her brief examination of my blood pressure and heart rate.

I had arrived from Pune with a friend whose name was Sakshin. We were FWBs, Friends With Benefits! Papaji spoke with him at the dinner table, while I just sat there on the floor like a stone Buddha. The only sign of life was those tears. The energy cylinder raged through me in my falling, gravity-less state, but my face was calm and even peaceful, according to eyewitnesses. The doctor accompanied Sakshin and me home in a rickshaw. By that time, about one hour had elapsed since it all started. I could move again but was still not talking. I rolled into bed and cried so deeply my whole body shook like crazy. It was as if a lifetime of sadness was leaving my heart and exiting my body all at once. I fell asleep exhausted from the whole ordeal.

The next morning I wearily opened my eyes, expecting to still feel funny. I was pleasantly surprised to find I did not. I sat up in bed, crossed my legs and closed my eyes again. Breathing deeply, I felt fresh, clear, happy and deeply calm. I was so relieved. In the meeting that morning – my first group meditation in Lucknow – Papaji called me to the front and asked me if I was okay. He wanted to know what I had experienced. As I had no clue, I found it hard to explain, but tried my best to do so, just as I am trying to do now! He told me that he believed it had been a healing on a very deep energy level. It had something to do with clearing negative karma from past lives. He was impressed and very happy for me to have had such an experience in his presence. Whatever it had been, the result was positive. I felt fantastic! He invited me to join him again for dinner that night. And so our relationship began, with great drama, through this extraordinary encounter.

When we meditate, all kinds of different things can happen. I have had many amazing experiences. It is best to not focus on the event itself, but rather on the overall benefits gained. It is easy to get caught up in wanting to have profound experiences every time one meditates, but this would be missing the point. Keep both feet firmly on the ground and seek only to be more grounded and peaceful in the now.

Being with Papaji was a magical time to which no words can do justice. I grew more confident about the path I was on under Papaji's amazing guidance. All his teachings pointed me firmly in the right direction and warned me to avoid all elements of New Age philosophies that promise achievement of peace and happiness sometime in the distant future after having done this, that or the other thing. This is the fallacy which makes many lose their way.

Freedom from suffering will only be found by awakening to this moment. I learnt that being good has nothing to do with being perfect. However, we can experience perfection through our self-acceptance. Some people might misunderstand "acceptance" and think that it means the same as adopting a defeatist attitude. Quite the contrary! Quickly accepting what can't be changed frees up energy for you to take action and focus on the things you can influence. We can't change our past, but we can choose how we will allow it to affect how we feel today. We can't change people, but we can decide what role, if any, they will play in our daily lives.

You may not learn how to be perfect, but you can learn how to live happily with your imperfections, with those of other people, and with those of the world. The funny thing is – when one can accept imperfections, one unwittingly creates perfection. Wise men say, "Everything is perfect just the way it is right now and just the way it is unfolding." When we look at the horrors in the world, then this seems like a bit of an unfair comment, right? How can babies being sexually abused or land mines blowing limbs off playing children be "everything unfolding perfectly?" This is a good question indeed. The thing to remember is that everyone has their own personal journey on this earth. Each person comes into this life with his or her own story to live out. Like actors in a movie, everyone seems to have a special role to play. Some people believe fate gave them their role. Others argue we chose this role at birth to learn something. At some point, free will determined how the roles and the characters will develop. I do not, by any means, claim to have the answer to the big question "Why?" Why is this person suffering so much more in this life than I am?

Religions try to answer this question with reincarnation theories. Some blame free will for the differences we see. Karma and other concepts are used to try to explain why some flourish and blossom while others wilt and perish without so much as a piece of bread or drink of water to keep them alive. Personally, I have yet to hear an explanation that has totally quenched my thirst for knowledge on this subject. They all seem sincere, yet dubious, attempts to explain something that just cannot be explained. I think the truth is, we just don't really know! It's one of those perplexing mysteries, like what happens to us when we die. I hate to believe that a suicide bomber really gets to enjoy sex with 100 virgins – or was it 1,000? Either way, you get my point! We have no clue what will happen to us when we die. We just hope it is something wonderful.

In the same way, we have no clue about why some people are born to experience tragedy or nightmarish lives while others seem to be particularly blessed with great fortune and love. All we have are theories and beliefs, yet no one can prove, with any certainty, any of the various beliefs. We will know death when we fully experience it. To me, being dead for a few minutes doesn't really count as fully dying. I think accounts from people who have died and come back to life are interesting. They don't give the full story, however, only a small part of what we could expect.

There are many different concepts out there. The truth is, we have no freaking clue, as much as we like to think we do! The mystery of death will be solved when we face death and find out what it is, and if there really is anything else on the other side. The "Why him and not me?" may also be realized through death, or it shall continue to be a mystery. Who knows? The point I want to make about all this is that your journey is yours and yours alone. Who really knows why it's turned out like this and not like that? The negative or positive unfolding of a life does not seem to follow any logical course or pattern. Good things can happen to bad people and bad things to good, as far as we can see.

My Personal Journey into Freedom

I have seen in my own life that my childhood, where I was the most helpless and vulnerable to other people's actions, has formed some strong aspects of good and bad in my personality. However, as an adult I have seen that my free will plays a large part in how my personality and life will continue to unfold. This means I am not a victim of my past because I am free to create my future in the now. I accept my past and refuse to carry it around with me everywhere I go like a heavy suitcase dragging on me and slowing me down. I accept the power to influence my future through my current thoughts and actions. I don't hang on to the hope of a better afterlife. It seems a big risk to take with the one brief life that's unfolding before me right now. I am committed to bringing heaven down to earth, as much as is humanly possible!

Papaji's teachings were exquisitely simple to me, yet supremely effective and deeply honest.

Keep quiet.

Stop seeking.

The only time is now.

You have to decide right now, once and for all, to be free.

Everyone who has ever found peace in this lifetime has made that decision.

I do not believe in a process of becoming. There is no goal at the end of a path of being. Freedom is here, now. Any sincere seeker will find this freedom in the now. Papaji never encouraged any notions or concepts of enlightenment being a process which needed time to achieve. Time is the very thing that keeps us in bondage and suffering and takes our attention away from the now.

Papaji: simple, clear, limitless and fantastically real.

The mother of all teachings came when I met Kai! Kai is my husband. At this writing we have been together for fourteen years. He may not be a spiritual teacher like Osho and Papaji, but what I learnt being with him is just as priceless and important.

Man, where to start? During my seven years between Chris and Kai being a single woman, I regularly toyed around with the idea of giving up sex all together. Yes, it is a long time to be single when you are still so young, right? I even wondered on more than one occasion if I was perhaps even a lesbian! That's how awkward most of the brief relationships with men were during that seven-year period. I did meet some super-sweet and charming guys, but something always went wrong or did not quite fit. Dating unsuccessfully for so many years can be grueling. What kept me sane? My unwavering trust that came from the positive energy I experienced through my meditations. I had discovered a remarkably lovable woman buried underneath the layers of quirky and fiery personality.

Sex was mostly complicated for me, so I felt nothing much would be lost if I did give it up for the more monastic approach. Maybe other people who do give up sex have similar issues with it, such as feeling that it takes more than it gives? But I totally abandoned these ideas of giving up sex after dating an English guy living in Australia who had studied Tantra under the strict guidance of the Western Tantric master Barry Long. He certainly was not the first man I met to claim knowledge in the art of Tantra. Some even called themselves Tantric masters! But Barry was certainly the first who really knew what he was doing! One guy's idea of being a Tantric master was roaring loudly like a wild lion during intercourse! Not fun at all, but hey, that could be just be my opinion. I imagine some women might actually love the sound of a man-lion roaring in their ears!

The Englishman brought my confused, sleeping body back to life through hours, days, weeks and months of extreme gentleness. He was filled with a beautiful determination and patience. Let me mention too his impressive discipline and complete mastery of his ejaculation. Any doubts concerning my sexual orientation were obliterated in the months we stayed together. Thank the Lord we met. I had obviously been worried that my feelings of sexual limitation had been due to the abuse from my stepfather. The Englishman explained to me that according to his teacher, many women have the same issues, even without ever having experienced any kind of sexual abuse. Barry Long believes that every woman has the ability to orgasm during sex. That it's just all about unlearning bad habits men and women develop around the sexual act. The trick is to be always honest with each other.

The truth will bring you closer together and help you make each other truly fulfilled sexually. Allowing women to be honest without men having a tantrum would seem like the obvious reaction, right? Wrong! Guys can get upset and despondent and withdraw sexually when faced with a woman's sexual frankness, and that makes women terrified to tell the truth. That is probably why at one point they just try to avoid sex as often as they can get away with it! Food for thought, guys. Give your woman the chance to say what is really going on with her when you make love, and take it like a man and have fun. Excuse the silly pun, people – I couldn't help myself.

As usual, everything was going better than I could have planned by the time I met Kai. I was a more sexually confident woman. We engaged in an honest dialogue about that from the beginning. Fourteen years into it and we are now having better, amazing, more mind-blowing sex than we did at the beginning of our relationship. I believe this is the result of years of honest discussions on the subject.

When Kai and I got together, it was clear from the first moments we started hanging out that this relationship was taking place on a different frequency from any others till that point. He wasn't doing my head in with complicated cat-and-mouse games. He knew what he wanted, and he loved self-development almost as much as I did. At the point we met, my life was pretty amazing. I knew who I was and what I wanted. I had an exciting life travelling around the world sharing inner peace and freedom with everyone and anyone who showed interest. I was able to work combining my two great passions: meditation and travelling.

When real love comes into your life, it may not look anything like you expected it to. That is why you need the wisdom to recognize it. The first three months of the romance with Kai were lovely. We were both on our best behaviour. Then, we started spending more time together, and that's when one starts to see the good and bad aspects of personalities. Some moments started to feel like open-heart surgery without the drugs that knock you out. I can see why most spiritual teachers prefer to go it solo, because the couple journey is definitely challenging. There is no way to get around that fact except, of course, through abstaining altogether, but trust me, that too will have its own set of challenges!

Centuries of bad habits between men and women, eons of cultural differences and millions of years of sexual frustration are working against us from the start. However, it is also a real test of unconditional love, and this is a very important point in self-development. Relationships are where you can truly get to practice what you preach. Love yourself and love your fellow man, even when he makes mistakes or does things that we can't – for the life of us – understand.

The rewards of breaking through the ego and discovering a pure love make the whole challenge totally worth it. Sharing oneself beyond the concealing mask of the ego is the most wondrous thing one can share with another human being. You will become totally vulnerable, but that vulnerability will become your strength. Most people get to experience this through the love of their children. It's just a pity they don't realize that this experience is also there to show us the depth and limitlessness of our ability to love ourselves and people other than our kids.

Kai and I were like two ships crossing in the night, and we almost missed meeting each other altogether. Sabine, the lady who is responsible for my third life-transforming meeting, had organized a four-day series of meditations for me in Hamburg. She told Kai that he really needed to make the effort to come out to one of the meetings and meet me.

I think she was trying to be a matchmaker for us. But on day four Kai still had not shown up to any meetings and I was leaving the next day to go to Amsterdam for more sessions. It was decided that we would go to an Indian restaurant to celebrate my last night in Hamburg, a Sunday in the fall. It was about ten that night that Sabine called Kai and tried to convince him that he really should get his butt off the couch and come over to the restaurant. He was having nothing to do with it. Even though the whole discussion took place in German, of which I did not speak a single word, I intuitively understood the whole thing. I have this strange ability to understand languages I don't speak when I really want to. For some reason I found myself grabbing the phone and saying no more than four words! Not "Hello, Kai, this is Mahima, blah blah blah". No, I just said, "You are coming, right?"

There was a long, intense silence and then a very cool voice answered, "Sure!" I handed the phone back to Sabine, smiling wickedly. And the rest, as they say, is history. Kai came to the restaurant, where nothing much happened. For me at least, there were no sparks or fireworks that night, or a marching band going off in my head when he entered the Taj Mahal restaurant looking a bit sleepy and worn out.

But fast forward to a few months later. I did feel a stirring somewhere, mmhmm! When he sashayed down the platform at the train station, John Travolta hips in white pants, wow! He was picking me up for the meditation sessions he had organized for me this time. It seems he had been impressed with me that night and had felt he had missed out on my last sessions in Hamburg, so invited me back. He had a big warm smile, which matched the beautiful bouquet of flowers he was carrying. He was wearing a luscious salmon-colored cashmere pullover and brown suede boots. I saw him in a totally different light. He now looked fresh, yummy, cute and irresistibly cuddly!

We spent many hours those first days just sitting together in silence, enjoying that we could share something so simple and yet so precious. It truly was beautiful. We took several months moving the relationship to a sexual one. We enjoyed long cuddles and kisses, of course. With such deep joyful meetings in silence and amazing conversations, we were not in a hurry. So we took our time.

Many couples these days make the mistake of diving into sex too soon. The sex may be great, but one will need a lot more than that to build a life together. Take your time to get to know if you even like each other, because once you open yourself up sexually, this will only impair your better judgment and ability to see clearly if you are truly compatible. It's hard to believe, but amazing sex can blind many into thinking they are in love!

What is even more important than great sex, you may ask? Can you really be happy in the day-to-day life with this person? Do you share the same basic principles, hopes, dreams and direction? That is what ultimately what will make the relationship more beautiful as time goes by and hence the sex too!

Our journey together has by no means been easy due to cultural differences and the simple fact that he is a man and I am a woman! However, it is incredibly fulfilling, nurturing, inspiring and an excellent source of learning and growing. I think what makes it work so well is that our relationships to ourselves have not gotten lost in the relationship with each other. Each needs to remain whole and responsible for their own happiness. We both feel blessed every day with what we already have. Everything else that comes into our lives is like the cherry on top of a fantastic sundae! It looks good, but you don't miss it or need it when it's not there.

If you would ask me what the three secrets to ensure everlasting love with your partner are, my answer would be, "1. Honesty, 2. Honesty, 3. Honesty!" Honesty allows you to be yourself with no games, no deception, no hiding or pretending to be something you are not. There is no trying to guess what the other is thinking or feeling, because you engage in open, direct, clear communication. Honesty is what keeps the trust and is the most intense thing to take from a partner, but it is also the very thing that will set you free and reduce your fear. Fear ruins everything in the end. Fear to face the truth will ruin your relationship. Fear to show who you really are can do the same.

Let's take the example of promiscuity in relationships, as this is an important factor for most couples and may come up at some point. If you talk often to each other in an open way about your sex life and about your feelings around the issue, chances are high outside adventures won't happen, especially if you say: "Darling, honestly, I need more sex and if we don't have it, I will need to find it somewhere else." Most people might not appreciate this kind of direct communication, but you can see how it could avoid the problem of husbands cheating on their wives or vice versa!

If we are not communicating honestly, we are hiding our real feelings, and those feelings will come out through our actions anyway, so why not express them and see what happens? We do not because we are afraid. We are afraid of where honesty may lead and what doors we may open with our honesty and how our partner will react to the truth. In this case, our partner could say something like, "Listen, dear, I really do love you but the amount of sex we have is plenty for me. Maybe you should find a mistress if you need more. You have my blessings! But don't give me details unless I ask and make sure you always use a condom!" I know many guys who would love a wife with this confidence!

When you are confident in what you share, you can accept the other for who they really are and not who you want them to be. Another response could be this: "Darling, I had no idea you were so frustrated. I am happy to make more of an effort to make sure we have more time for each other. I appreciate your honesty". There is no wrong answer when you just tell the truth, not what you think the other person wants to hear. Honesty is a tricky energy, as we never know what reaction we may get! You can be sure, however, that you will most likely get an honest response to an honest statement. This will save you a lot of frustration and time in the long run.

I think this truth concept can be used to improve all relationships, even work relationships. The secret is to make sure it's the truth of your heart and not your ego. Be clear that I am not talking about using honesty as a way to be rude and insensitive to other people's feelings. If you speak from the heart, you will know the difference and use honesty correctly and with sensitivity. If you can love yourself fully as you are, right now, then you can love another in the same way. And you will also be comfortable having them really see you as you are and not as they want you to be. As much as people should love us for who we are right now, just as much do we need to aspire to be the best we can be in the now.

When you love yourself, you know you are not perfect. So why would you demand perfection from the other? Truth will help you get through the challenging times. It's the truth that will keep you laughing with each other and loving each other, one moment at a time. It will set you free and allow you to live in the reality. Even if the truth is not always easy to take or give, its effect on our happiness in the long run is powerful.

I can't claim to know what the future has in store for the Kai and Mahima saga, but what I can say without a shadow of a doubt is that some of the life lessons I have been able to learn through this relationship are priceless! For that I will always be grateful. I think the greatest lesson to master in any relationship is an unconditional love through forgiveness. One has to forgive oneself for not always being able to react the way one would like to. One has to forgive oneself for not being perfect. You will also have to learn to forgive the other person for whatever mistakes they will make due to the same problem. Yes, what they do during these times may seem unforgivable. Yet the truth is that everything can be forgiven, if not forgotten, because the heart has that great capacity!

As we grow personally, our relationships should also grow and get better and smoother. If that is not the case, then something is wrong. In your inner circle be only with people who are interested in continuing to learn and grow and be better human beings. With people like this in your life you will discover the real joy in relating.

Kai has especially taught me how to deal with human love, through honesty, integrity and patience. I am beautifully challenged, every single day, to put into practice what I preach. Mastering unconditional love by staying open, gentle and loving.

Sexuality And Enlightenment

After my first experience of deep inner peace, it soon became very clear to me that if I kept my daily focus on being loving and peaceful in the here and now, nothing else really mattered. Everything else would work itself out without my worry, stress and concern. It's like finding the key to the meaning of your life and knowing you can't be locked out ever again because you have that key. A deep relaxation comes into you, yet at the same time you are fully engaged and living more intensely and passionately than you did before.

How we think about and deal with sex will affect how we feel about ourselves. It's worth taking a deeper look into your sexual attitude and making peace with it. That is why I believe it is important to remember this: the attitude of "I am giving up sex, giving up men, giving up women, giving up this and that, in order to find God, to be closer to God" may just be another very clever place for your ego to hide and grow and keep you in its prison of limitation. You may argue that many spiritual teachers have let go of sex, so it must be the ideal way and we should all aspire to do the same. I would argue that besides this being very old school, why should we give up something as natural as sex? What would be a good enough reason? I for one can't think of any! It would be like giving up using your arms or your legs with the idea that doing so will bring you closer to God. That would be clearly insane, right? Yet when it comes to the issue of sex, we lose all sense of rational thinking. The body gives up sex in its own time as we age, so just let nature run its course!

In the past, teachers earned more respect when they were seen to be doing things that were beyond the capabilities of the ordinary man or woman. Creating miracles in one way or the other, abstaining from sex, making the blind see again or turning water to wine. People wanted their teachers to be demigods. Even today there are many teachers who are believed to have supernatural powers. I think that it is great to show us the limitless power of the human being, yet we should not lose touch with the fact that more important than developing the ability to perform miracles is developing the ability to be peaceful, peace-loving and compassionate human beings. That's how we will stop building cleverer bombs and guns to kill each other, training bigger armies to fight each other, bullying each other in schools and mobbing each other at work and online. That is what the world needs more of: ordinary people becoming extraordinary by living with higher levels of compassion and integrity. The greatest leaders of our time have been very human. People like "The King" (Martin Luther King) and Nelson Mandela never laid claim to any supernatural powers and yet they have greatly influenced and changed our world for the better. Through their great passion and profound courage they have become superb examples of a modern enlightened mind.

We need to evolve our relationship with sex and spirituality into a more balanced and non-conflictive one. In this new era, it is my sincere hope that all spiritual teachers will change their attitudes and personal practices and drop celibacy and being single. This lifestyle choice leads to so many unanswered questions about their honesty around the subject, which in turn leads to confusion among their students as they struggle to deal with their own sexuality in a positive way. It is time to include practical advice and lead by example by integrating their philosophies to include dealing with human nature on a moment-to-moment basis. It is my belief that teachers need to show us that even with husbands, children and work pressures, we can all still rise to the challenge and live peaceful, happy and enlightened lives. If they can't do that, are they really good role models for today's men and women? Or are they just perpetuating the unhealthy relationships we have with sex and with each other?!

There is no denying that sex is not always practiced in a positive way, but the belief that sex is somehow something we should feel ashamed of and need to drop altogether (if we are to reach high levels of spiritual enlightenment) can't be the right way either.

Do we really want to live in a world where everyone is single because we don't know how to live happily and peacefully together? You may well ask, "Well, dreamer, do you think we should all get married and try to live happily ever after?" I think everyone should do whatever feels right for them; however, I also strongly feel if we are going to lead others, then surely it must be through example. Anyone who claims the knowledge of self-awareness ought to show us how to fully integrate that knowledge with everyday living in the twenty-first century.

The Question of Discipline

We need to start educating ourselves positively through open discussions about the basic human drives and needs that are still part of modern-day culture and society. That includes reflecting on what we eat and the way we have sex, what we think about all forms of drugs and the way we deal with alcohol. Intuitively we all know what is right for us as individuals, and if we could get past our denial, we would find a healthier, more balanced way to interact with these things. In the spiritual culture, we seek perfection in how we deal with sex, food, drugs and alcohol as a proof of advanced spiritual achievement. The truth of the matter, as is clearly seen in the world around us, is this: even if someone does not drink alcohol, takes no drugs, has sex only with their partner and eats only vegetarian food, that does not automatically make them a happier, more peaceful, loving and compassionate human being. However, they are probably going to have very healthy bodies from the clean diet and lack of drugs and alcohol!

From my years of working with people and meditation, I can tell you what I have observed: being very disciplined with these things makes little difference in the long run on a person's level of thoughtfulness, emotional intelligence, compassion or ability to be happy and peaceful in the now. If anything, these lifestyle choices can feed the ego, building a feeling of superiority and arrogance, causing some people to become heavily judgmental towards others because they drink alcohol or eat meat. Some people just use discipline to feed their egos, while the truth is they continue to cause themselves and those around them to suffer.

The human evolution I speak of is not about putting yourself into a box and thinking you are better than everyone else because you live in a certain way. We already have that kind of thinking in abundance, and it clearly does not work towards creating more harmony among different cultures, societies and ethnic groups.

We need to be free thinkers, authentic individuals who look beyond what someone eats, drinks, smokes or whatever as a way to judge their character. Surely how they conduct themselves on a daily basis, what they say, do and how they treat other people, should hold more value than the rest. There is no doubt that disciplining our vices is a virtue worth putting into action and practice daily, yet when embarking on a path to self-discovery, one should not lose focus of what really counts: spreading peace, positivity and joy to loved ones and total strangers alike. You will need to seriously question yourself to develop a healthy relationship with your body and what you put into it – that goes without saying. Authenticity with how one chooses to interact with sex, food, drugs and alcohol is important. It's all about finding a healthy way and respecting each other's individual choices. Having said that, I will now emphasize how important it is to educate yourself on how mass meat production is negatively affecting our planet. Reducing meat in the diet would be well advised. Please do not let the discipline factor stop you from making the effort to connect to yourself in a deeper and more positive way; the rest will fall into place, as it is true for you and as you get more in touch with yourself and learn to truly listen to, obey and respect your body.

An Ordinary Life

While living in Pune those first six months of my meditation journey, I came to a clear realization regarding how I wanted to live my new lease on life. I decided I wanted to be independent and not have to work for anybody other than myself. I had no idea how I was going to do that, but I just knew that's what I wanted to manifest in my life.

My heart has always clearly guided me, and I have not compromised my dreams or my principles in the pursuit of money. Being happy means the world to me, and life is just too short to live in misery! I want it all, no compromising. Work I love, living in places I adore, with people I enjoy and enough money to travel, shop, share and have a good time. You get what you ask for and what you believe you deserve, so be careful and clear what you wish for. Somehow this attitude of believing I deserve the very best has proven again and again to be a magnet for good experiences. Money has always manifested at exactly the right moments I needed it to fuel my passion and creativity.

In the 90s, meditation was still an abstract concept in Western culture. Many people just did not get why sitting silently and learning to master their mind and emotions would be of any long-lasting value. Even now it can hardly be described as a mainstream activity. Most people still have a somewhat negative association with meditation, until they try it, of course, and then they love it! The widespread idea that it is really hard to meditate is a sad misperception. Yoga helps to create a more accepting and open mind towards meditation. I hope to contribute to changing people's attitudes about it, as it truly is one of the most effective ways to relieve stress, get focused on positivity and become more easygoing and flexible in the now. Yoga is taking over Western gyms as people feel themselves spiraling faster and faster out of control and mental balance.

With high levels of stress and burnout syndrome on the rise, we need to find solutions. We are more open to Eastern ideas and preventive medicines as the Western options are becoming scarier. Valium and other addictive pills are prescribed and popped left, right and center. You don't have to be an outcast, hippy, revolutionary or black sheep to start wondering whether there are other alternatives to how we live. Inner peace and freedom are easier to have than many assume. My thoughts over the decades have condensed down into simple steps. Three of them, to be precise. Let me present you with some wonderful alternative ways of thinking and feeling. I believe that by implementing these three simple steps into your daily life routine, you will take a quantum leap into a happier and more peaceful and passionate you.

FIRST STEP: "WHO AM I?"

This question is a perfect place to start. It's the first thing you will need to consider when looking to liberate yourself from your own personal suffering and connect to more peace, love and happiness in your daily life. When we know who we are, the world becomes a much friendlier, warmer place. However, before we tackle this important question, it is important to understand why one should focus on finding not just mental peace, but also love and true happiness. When you engage in all three disciplines, it will keep you on your toes and keep your attention on what really matters.

Peace, love and happiness do interact and interconnect with one another, and one may lead to the other. There are, however, three essential elements to consider separately. Peace of mind is relatively easy to master quickly with the right teacher and guidance. Love and happiness are altogether different disciplines, because they involve interaction with other people, cultures, societies and the world in general. Start with finding peace from your mental activity and the roller-coaster ride of your emotions. This is done by understanding your deeper nature beyond your name and physical body, hence the question "Who am I?" When you have come to understand more about the "I" in the question "Who am I?" you will know that you are not just that. This realization that you are more than the "I" allows you to have more of an advantageous bird's-eye view of your thoughts and feelings. This experience of more peace will lead you to realize that love also needs to be added to the mix if you do not want to become a recluse or outcast living a peaceful but lonely life. Rejecting the world and everything and everyone in it can become a side effect of just focusing on your own peace of mind. The awareness of the importance of unconditional love will allow you to have more compassion and empathy for others without losing your own connection to inner peace.

Just because someone is unhappy or suffering doesn't mean you have to also feel the same to empathize with them. You can still be compassionate and have great empathy for others while staying connected to your own peacefulness and joy. Love will help you open up and make life more about sharing, relating and interacting. However, we must not be attached to this sharing and we must not put a prison wall around the people we love. It is not the work of our kids, friends, or spouses to make us feel happy; that's our own responsibility. They may try with all their might, but will fail miserably if we are not ready to be happy, to stop being unhappy.

Peace is what you will experience when you stop thinking. Love is there to help us take part in the human experience. Happiness is what you choose to be every day, when you realize through peaceful, loving compassion that the world needs your positive energy through your thoughts, feelings and actions. In seeking great wisdom, you will realize that there is no end to what is possible. Do not look for an end to learning or growing. This humble attitude will keep you open and kind.

Now back to the all-important question: "Who am I?" This question has so often been answered by wise men and women with a warm smile, a long deafening silence, then the whimsical yet still beautiful answer of "I am that!" And I am that and that and that and that and that and that multiplied by infinity! Let's go deeper into it, or if you feel you already got it, feel free to skip to the next step. Just kidding! You are going to love what you read next – it's gently mind expanding.

I have worked with many privileged people who have all the comforts one could need and yet are restless, unhappy, super-stressed and out of balance with themselves and the world around them. Can you relate to this? Privilege to me is not about being a billionaire, millionaire or a super-rich person. I evaluate privilege by my African roots and background. Privileged, by my standards, is the following: anyone living with running water that they can drink directly from the tap without getting sick, having a real bed to sleep in and a home with electricity, a fridge with food in it and medical assistance around the corner or in the next village when needed – this is privileged. To be privileged also means living in a place with no bombs going off in the distance and no soldiers and/or rebels running through the town killing everything that moves. Being privileged means living under a government that has no mad dictator terrorizing the masses and having a currency that is relatively stable. Having a decent job that allows you to earn money to cover your monthly expenses is a privilege. You would be surprised to find out just how many privileged people there are in the world. Sadly, there are not as many as there should be.

Are you privileged? You decide. It takes honesty to recognize the blessings bestowed upon oneself. Do you believe that your life is complicated and really challenging? Is your life really difficult to cope with, or is it just the way you view reality, along with your attitude that can make life seem even harder than it really is or needs to be? Don't overthink it. The truth is – yes! Your attitude and perspective do have a huge impact on how miserably, or not, you will experience life. When you are connected to the deeper reality beyond the ego point of view, you will see your life in relationship to what's going on in the world around you. The two will not be separate. This means that even when you can't see something happening right in front of your eyes, it does not make it irrelevant or less a part of your daily reality.

It is like having access to a bird's-eye view. But imagine the bird is flying in space looking down on earth, able to see everything that is going on down here in the world in one glance. Imagine you are that bird. How hard does your daily reality look from that perspective, now that you can appreciate and see other people's realities? Can you see how your perception could change your attitude when you see things from this angle? The way we see ourselves will greatly affect how we feel in this world.

Maybe a couple of weeks in an African village or Asian slum with no real toilets, no clean drinking water for miles around and no food in the fridge because there is no electricity would give you a taste of how good your life and reality really is. Walking in those shoes even for a minute would make you feel more content and grateful for the things you take for granted. Complaining constantly about your life may start to seem like an arrogant person's luxury sport.

The same life that previously seemed hard and difficult before you took the bird's-eye view may seem like a blessed life! Your life is the same, but your perspective has changed. That's really what this book is all about – changing your perspective to connect you to a more peaceful and joyful you in the here and now, no matter where you come from and what your reality is right now in this moment. What about the poor people in those slums? How should they cope with the lack of balance and fairness in this world? Which perspective should they take to feel happier and more peaceful in the now? A very good question indeed! From my personal experience, I have seen that self-awareness is available and accessible to anyone and everyone who is tired of suffering and ready to reconnect to inner peace.

Some people think that the seeking of self-knowledge, inner bliss and peace is the luxury of people from middle-class to upper-class societies. How absurd is that?! They even think it is wrong to tell someone who has very little material wealth that joy and peace lie within one's own heart. The funny thing is that often those people with little material wealth will tell you themselves that real joy and peace lies within our own hearts. The peace and inner joy that I speak of truly has no connection to what's going on in anyone's financial and material life at this or any moment in time. It is an experience that is beyond the coming and going of money, health, relationships or all the things we give importance to as factors that contribute to and create happiness within us.

Every human being is born already connected to this energy, or to God, if you prefer that word. At some point during the transition from child to adult, the ego gets in the way and interferes with our ability to stay connected to this inner realm of positivity, love and happiness. Everyone has the right to reconnect and find the way back to that greater intelligence, regardless of where one is in the world and regardless of whatever state one's life, health or wealth is in. No matter who you are, how you live, or what's going on around you right now, know that if you seek internal peace from personal suffering, you will find it. You can discover a peaceful sanctuary within. This inner place is part of this world. Even though it is not visible to the eye, it can be experienced and seen directly through the heart. It is a place where incredible energy, majestic beauty and breathtaking stillness can be experienced as clearly as the sun kissing your face or the wind blowing through your hair. The awakening to this inner state of being has been called "enlightenment" by some. Others believe it is the experience of having a direct conversation and connection to God. Some believe it is getting in touch with one's Buddha nature. I like to call this awakening "being yourself".

When you experience it – even if just for a moment – you will then fully realize the true madness of thinking that such an experience has anything to do with outer life circumstances. Even a person of poverty and terrible life conditions can reach in and acquire access to this type of freedom, if that is what they seek. Awakening to deep peace and profound love is possible for us all and is not class exclusive. It does not depend on whether you are full or hungry, dirty or clean, rich or poor. In fact, in the past, some people would give up all their possessions in their quest and hunger to connect to this state of deep peace and inner bliss. They believed that jobs, relationships, money and so forth were distractions which they did not need while seeking this inner state of abundance. This happened and still happens in India, where this kind of holy men and women walk through the streets almost naked. People support them by giving them food and water, believing that this lifestyle is better suited for seeking and acquiring deep peace and lasting happiness.

Some say that it is easier to find freedom from the ego and mind when unburdened by worldly possessions and comforts. I am not saying I agree or disagree, but I am using this as, hopefully, a convincing argument. So, people of the upper class and middle class can please stop saying this: "It's easy to talk about peace, love, integrity, happiness when our bellies are full and we have all the basics we need to be happy and fortunate". This may be true when seeking superficial levels of happiness, but real inner peace is more about the individual than his bank account or possessions.

Inner peace does not care how rich or poor or educated or uneducated you are. Yet the higher the level of intellect, you will often find the higher the level of concern that it is not right to talk to poor people about inner peace and happiness.

Are we saying the poorest of us have earned the right to not be too concerned with their actions because life has dealt them a shitty hand for reasons nobody really knows? Are we saying they should feel free and justified to fight, steal, rape, be corrupt, miserable and indulge in whatever negative actions they feel like? That because of their situation they should seek neither happiness nor peace, or try to better themselves? Are we saying that because they are born in poverty and hardship we do not have the right to ask them to reflect on their attitude or question how their thoughts, words and actions could be contributing to their reality? Come now! We know that humans may not have been born equal in the material world; however, in a world with any integrity, men and women have equal rights and abilities, if they so choose, to rise to heights of great inner wisdom, powerful compassion and spiritual intelligence. They just need to know, as we all need to know, that this option is available.

With our ability to wake up to real and lasting inner peace, all can seek and find personal freedom, and who knows which environment is more suited for this quest? So, let's stop with the whole "it's easy to talk about peace when we live in great abundance". Yes, it's crazy and egotistical to not feel grateful for your abundance but also to believe that it is material abundance that "makes the man". I can't imagine what it must be like to have very little to smile about. I also can't imagine a human being born without the choice to take responsibility for how they act, think and feel regardless of their outer circumstances. Free will gives each person the freedom to notice how their actions, thoughts and words affect the world around them and to do something about that.

Who we are inside matters. It directly affects the world we live in. Who we are in the material world matters less than what kind of human being we are inside. People in countries of great poverty suffer because of a lack of integrity in their government leaders. They also suffer from the cruelty of the people living among them in poverty – many of whom have turned to extreme violence as a way of life.

Add that to their own personal suffering and yes, their situation is tough. Yet it is for this exact reason that personal freedom and inner peace are so important for them to reconnect to. I am also sure that there are many amazing people trying desperately to help their fellow man in these poorest countries but whose efforts go unnoticed due to the high levels of greed and corruption which happen when large sums of money are involved. We can never stop doing good just because we think nothing is changing. The change may not be obvious, but things are evolving for the better as more and more people question their individual contribution to the way things are.

No matter where an individual comes from and what ill fate or great fortune has been bestowed upon them, they can choose to rise like a phoenix from the ashes of their ego and claim their freedom to be a loving, peace-filled being. Ego will greatly distort what we see, feel and think. Find out who you are in the deeper core, beyond the ego and the obvious such as name, sex, age, occupation and status. Find this out and you will find freedom.

I will tell you who you are beyond the ego and what answers lie behind the question "Who am I?", but without your fully accepting the idea of ego as limiting and integrating this truth into the way you see yourself, this knowledge will not help you free yourself from your ego. It really only comes to life when you can admit that beyond the ego lies a more wise and peace-loving you.

The ego is what stands between you and your core self. The ego is like the flesh on an apple. It's the seeds that make the apple immortal. So the seed is really the core of what an apple is. The flesh may be sweet, bitter, soft and mushy, or crisp and crunchy. All apples are different and yet they all share one truth. In every apple there is a core with seeds, and those seeds can give apples endless possibilities.

I want to use this analogy to describe to you the way I experience other human beings, and also to help you understand the question

"Who am I"? We share the same tuth as an apple, in that while we are all different on the outside, in the core we are all the same.

Our true nature is beyond the flesh, blood, organs and bones. Our true nature gives us endless possibilities of growth, flexibility, compassion and connectivity. When one fully realizes the limiting nature of the ego, this is known as an awakening, a self-realization. This awakening will bring yu true self-confidence and deeper integrity, as well as building a strong connection to peace and contentment in the here and now.

The most effective and deliberate way I know to awaken and be released from the limitations of the ego is through meditation. We can also call it self-contemplation, sitting silently, or my personal favorite, "Love Silence". People get terrified just hearing the word meditation, and that's why I think it is important to define what that really is, to deterrorize it somehow. Through silence we can still the mind, and it is when the mind is still that the connection to this inner place of peace, love and happiness can be rediscovered.

Meditation: What Is It Really All About?

Is meditation an ancient technique used by special people like celibate monks and priests to converse with the Almighty? Yes and like yoga, its roots are steeped in old traditions. And yet it is now widely practiced all over the world regardless of religious beliefs. Everyone can enjoy and benefit from meditation. Meditation as a discipline of its own is finally making its way into mainstream thinking and already being effectively used to transform the lives of ordinary men and women. There is now also a lot of scientific evidence that highlights the special effects of meditation on the brain, as well as its abilities to help us focus and to reduce symptoms of stress. It is worth Googling to find out more of the fascinating scientific facts about meditation and the effects it has on us.

We now know that at least eighty-five percent of all diseases are stress related. So knowing how to calm down, relax and detach has never been more relevant than it is right now. As the world moves forward at a faster pace, stress levels are rising every year, with burnout and depression being top problems for employees.

Meditation gave me access to a confidence and inner strength that I wish everyone could have the pleasure of experiencing. It may be a solemn and ancient technique used by celibate monks and Buddhists, but it is also a very effective power tool for anyone who wants to overcome the many challenges of modern life. Let your fear of meditation go. It really just means sitting silently. Sitting and not talking, observing the coming and going of thoughts, feelings and breath. Getting your focus out of time and into the here and now. Connecting to a peace that comes to one effortlessly when one lets go of the thinking mind, time, past, future and ultimately the physical body. In a nutshell, meditation develops your ability to let go of negative emotions and thoughts and just be.

Death of The Ego

Death of the ego is liberation from a limited mental point of view in which one believes that one is only the I – the body and the mind. The ego is what causes your unhappiness and disconnectedness. It is responsible for your feelings of being lost, alone, confused, unloved, afraid, hopeless, helpless, depressed, stressed, frustrated, angry, jealous, bitter and anything else negative you can think of. Feel free to add to this list! Anytime that you experience these strong negative emotions, you can be sure that the ego is at the centre of it, and until you confront your ego, you will not feel released from the negativity these emotions create.

What Exactly is The Ego?

The ego is our personality. It is the sum of our upbringing and the beliefs our society has taught us about right and wrong. Beliefs are powerful things that make us act and think in a certain way. Beliefs such as "men are the designated heads of the family", or "baby boys are more valuable than baby girls" are perfect examples of how the ego uses its limited view to control and dominate in a way that does not necessarily serve the greater integrity of humanity.

It is a mask you put on so the world will see you in a certain way. There can be much self-importance and unawareness when people operate from this place. That's when we see conflicts that escalate into violence and seem to have no solutions or possibilities to meet in the middle. That's when we see people's human rights stripped away, while ideals are followed which are not based in equality and fairness.

Ego separates you from your true nature, which is peaceful, loving and compassionate. We all know this on some deep level, no matter how far off that path we may have strayed. Look at how good the ego is at destroying our planet while maintaining an inhumane distance between rich and poor.

Me, myself and I – these three fools can make your life hell on earth if you allow them to dictate how you live your life. The ego is what we see manifesting as abuse of women, extreme poverty, irresolvable conflict, corruption, terrorism and "I am right-ism". Yes, there is an I in right, but also in fight, which is where always needing to be right leads us!

The ego even makes us believe our religion is better than everyone else's. Our God is the one and only, our culture is the best and right way. Rather than just embracing the positive in each other, it came to be that we get stuck on debating and fighting about who's right and who's wrong, thereby losing the point of integrity and love that all religions are desperately trying to instill in us in the first place. The ego will stop one from confronting one's own religious beliefs that may have become outdated, backward, controlling and even dubious. Beliefs like "it is a sin to be gay" or "women are not pure enough or clean enough to hold powerful positions in religious organizations".

On a personal level, one's ego might find it hard to say something as simple as " I am sorry, I was wrong", or "Yes, I made a terrible mistake, forgive me". The ego could even make saying "I love you" feel like a visit to the dentist! Showing one's love, affection and vulnerability seems like a weakness. The ego wants you to keep vulnerable feelings a closely guarded secret, and "Please, no tears! For goodness sake, you are a grown man! Pull it together!" and "Women, no crying in the boardroom! You will lose face showing real uncensored emotion like that!"

It is when our ego blocks us from bringing joy to others with our actions and words that it goes too far. I love this quote from Will Smith: "If you are not making someone else's life better, then you are wasting time!" It speaks to me because I believe it is our very purpose in this world to bring joy to others. We would pretty much allow the ego to get away with murder if it meant we got to continue hiding behind it. The trouble is, the ego wins, but *you* lose.

A lovely gentlemen once told me a simple but rather sad story about how he asked an old lady who had trouble walking if she needed any help up a flight of stairs. There was no elevator in that building. She looked surprised and was delighted to accept his kind helping hand. He had a tear in his eyes when he told me this story because as they mounted the stairs the woman confessed that no one had ever offered her assistance before and she appreciated it so very much.

He looked in my eyes with his wet eyes and said, "Where are we going with all this, Mahima, if we can't even show our caring in these simple acts of kindness?!"

The ego is only concerned with itself and does not have time to waste on random acts of kindness or sensitive consideration for other people's feelings, especially people we don't even know. It has much more important things to do, places to go, people to see, things to accomplish at whatever cost. If we can liberate ourselves from the limitations of the ego, we will become one more light in the world, contributing to more harmony and to less selfishness, jealousy, envy, greed, anger and fear. There will be more helpful hands reaching out to that "older lady".

Becoming Yourself, Self-realization and
Enlightenment

Now that you know what the ego is all about, let me tell you more about who you are at the core and how you can escape the seductive clutches of the ego. Remember, it's the first step on the path to more happiness and peace in the here and now.

Who you are is beyond gender and name. It is the energy that connects everything and exists in everything. It's the part of you that can never die. You are always connected to it and can never be separated from it. You can only believe that you are separated from it through the mind and ego. We just need to become conscious of this connection to start benefiting from it in our daily lives.

We connect to the world through the physical body and our thoughts. The body is like a cup holding this essence. There are many words that have been given to describe this essence, such as love, God, Buddha nature, chi, source, energy, light, soul or spirit. I don't care what you prefer to call it, but I will refer to it as energy or source. When you connect to this part of yourself, you will find a love that knows no bounds, a joy that is independent of circumstance, an ability to be present in the now. It is like plugging into a limitless power supply. Think of the great adventurers of the world and all the incredible things they do, like running a naked and barefoot marathon at the North Pole. These people perform feats that would kill an ordinary human being. They are tapping into this powerful part of themselves that has limitless potential, energy and knowledge. We all have access to this energy and you have tapped in and out of it many times in your own life without consciously choosing to do so. At the moments when you felt invincible, powerful, overjoyed or bubbling with creativity or found yourself "in the zone", you were connecting to that greater part of yourself. Meditation is the conscious choice to plug in to that energy source.

I am strongly encouraging you, if you have not already done so, to take the time to make that deeper connection to yourself. Awareness of who you really are needs to happen in every moment, and there will never be a better time than now to start! The good news is that even a small amount of practice will go a long way.

Every day you must realize that you are not the ego, not the body, not your relationships, not your possessions, not your money and not your emotions and thoughts. When you look with an open heart, you will see that the truth is that you came into this world with nothing and you will leave with nothing.

When you can fully accept this undeniable truth deep within your consciousness and live daily with this awareness, the suffering you experience in your life will become much less. Much of our suffering is self-created through not being able to let go and "go with the flow". You will become more relaxed and you will see life more as an interesting and exciting adventure, full of unexpected twists and turns. Shift your focus away from the physical body and connect to the deeper core that is your true nature. Freedom, joy and peace will become second nature to you when you take time every single day to shine a light on your ego and get in touch with that greater energy in you.

How to Start Being Connected to This Greater Part of Yourself

Please note that as a beginner, meditating on your own will be harder than in the presence of a teacher who can point you and guide you in the right direction. It's like learning to drive a car. You may be able to teach yourself (this is extremely rare), but it would be so much easier and less scary if you got someone who already knows how to drive to teach you. That way you can ask questions and make faster progress. Join a meditation group, or do some private training in meditation with a teacher.

I always find it amusing when people say they prefer meditating on their own. To me, meditation is like dancing. It can be great to dance alone in your room, but it's just so much better to dance with someone or in a group. The experience is just so beautiful when you get into harmony with, or on the same wavelength as, another human being – or a whole group. Ultimately being able to enjoy both meditating alone and with others is what I would advise anyone to aim for. Both offer something very special and necessary.

Make sure when choosing a group that there is a good teacher you like, but also know that your ego might be obstructing your view. Make sure you attend a few classes before deciding if the group is helpful or not. The same will apply when you try private lessons. Do a few lessons before deciding if the teacher is right unless, of course, you have an intense "Hell no!" towards the teacher or group from day one. Trust your intuition, but don't give up. Keep going till you find the right teacher and group. It will be well worth the effort. We spend so much of the very little precious time we have on this planet trying to escape ourselves. The problem is that while we may escape getting in touch with what we are really feeling and what we really want from life, we are also blocking our possibility to experience the real inner peace and happiness which is our birthright.

Ego is not something talked about as much as love, equality, justice and freedom, yet it is the one thing that stands in the way of us experiencing all these other things on a much grander scale. Because it is not that much talked about, our egos can get in the way of our personal growth pretty fast if we don't take extra care to make sure that does not happen. When we find ourselves commenting frequently and with great intensity about how stupid this person is, or what a terrible arsehole that person is, we might want to make sure we are walking our talk and being the change we want to see in the world. Otherwise we are all just hypocrites, right? It is easy to point a finger of blame and disgust while we hardly look at how we might be guilty of some form of uncool behaviour or thinking. After all, none of us is perfect. The thing is, when you stop blaming your boss for your misery, you empower yourself to take back your power and do something to change the situation. If you believe you deserve better, you will find the courage to act on that belief.

We can so easily judge others instead of being focused on taking responsibility for how our words, actions and thoughts are affecting the people around us. Do we bring them peace and joy or are we just sulky spoilt brats that don't know how to be happy and peaceful even with all the benefits and comforts we may have? Don't worry if you think you might be a sulky spoilt brat! Just becoming aware of it will go a long way and will definitely get the ball rolling in the right direction. Awareness of ourselves is the key to overcoming aspects of our personality that we have learnt but which no longer serve us or support us to be who we want to be in the now.

I must share this funny story about how I had an almost fatal run-in with my ego after I had been in India for about nine months. It was with my second teacher, Papaji. He confronted my ego in one of the meditation sessions in front of everybody. He mocked me and teased me so badly the whole hall was in stitches. In this case they were definitely laughing at me as opposed to with me! At least that is what it felt like to my ego!

I had written a letter asking him why some of the people in his close inner circle were so aggressive. Often when you went to his house, a tough character greeted you with bared teeth at the front gate, snapping at you in harsh tones, eyes glaring rudely. When you finally got permission to enter the house, you felt that if looks could kill, you would be dead on the spot with your eyes closed and pretending not to notice. Having never been with any other living spiritual teacher before, I had no idea why these people were behaving so badly (in my eyes) when they were living so close to such a powerful source of positivity and light.

I still don't really get it, but ultimately, what was I there for? To liberate myself from my personal suffering, or to continue to put my focus on the others, trying to understand the politics of his setup? I was judging and criticizing them instead of just focusing on myself and overcoming my own shortcomings. Beware of being overly concerned about what other people are doing or are not doing, as this activity does tend to reinforce your own ego and increase feelings of superiority and arrogance.

Whenever we feel superior to other people, whether it be emotional, intellectual, or even spiritual superiority, we are in the ego, and our ability, to connect, empathize, share, learn and grow becomes greatly compromised. You cannot learn something from people you think you are better than. Everybody can teach you something. Even a person who cannot read and write may teach you something deep, profound and life transforming. If your ego is in the way and all you see is an uneducated person, you may not be open to receive the gifts that person may have to share with you. Even the bad and terrible events in our lives teach us something. These experiences can awaken us when seen from a different vantage point. They are gifts for our personal development and can greatly empower us.

So there I was in a meeting with over a hundred people, all rolling in laughter! It probably did not happen quite that harshly in reality, but it felt like people were cheering Papaji on to put me in my place good and proper! Papaji had my letter in his hand, the letter I had written that asked him why the people around him were not more kind, warm and welcoming.

Let me just go back for a moment to another thing that happened months before I had grown the balls to actually write that letter. Papaji's right-hand man had threatened to beat me up during my first week in Lucknow because I had, without getting permission from the right-hand man's wife, entered a small side room where Papaji was meeting with people after the main meeting in the hall. She was posted as a guard at the door making sure only the invited people went inside. I asked her if I could go in but she said no, for whatever reason, so I decided to just brush past her. During that meeting Papaji invited me to come and sit with him and we had a good chat, plus he invited me to be a regular for dinner at his home in the evenings. For anyone who knows the Lucknow setup, this was a big deal! His house was tiny and space was limited; it was an honor bestowed on few. It was an invitation to be part of his inner circle. Well worth the risk I had taken by just cheekily and impulsively inviting myself into the room. The next thing I knew, directly after Papaji had left the small room, the husband asked to talk to me. We walked away from the crowds of people who were joyfully waving goodbye to Papaji's car. He suddenly grabbed my arm roughly, taking me by surprise. He looked at me menacingly, saying if I ever did that again he would beat me up. He definitely wiped the "happy to be invited to the inner circle" grin off my face. The whole experience was quite upsetting, but I was still happy I had just followed my own feeling and entered the room anyway. I share this with you only so you can understand better why I found myself in that awful position. I must always speak up against what feels wrong to me. Being threatened by this guy and some other stuff I had witnessed at his house and around the hall put the question inside my heart, and it would not go away! By the time this all had happened, including the reading of my letter, I had already been in Lucknow for three months. In those three months I had never asked Papaji any questions related to meditation, self-realization or enlightenment.

So he had seen me sitting there in his meetings month after month, just listening, learning and absorbing everything that I could from him. And then when I finally did open my mouth, it was not to share something about my own truth or ask a meaningful question to go deeper, but rather to judge and question what was going on around him. Now just to be clear, Papaji actually loved my letter – so much so, according to someone who was there, that he got everyone in his inner circle to read it and reflect on their behavior! He fully acknowledged my letter to be true. I think it was fear that drove them to act like they did. Whenever fear is present, we react in a different way – less peaceful, less loving. Whatever their reasons were, was it really any of my concern? Why was I in Lucknow, really?

Papaji took the only opportunity I had presented him with to push me to go deeper. He decided to expose my ego in front of everybody. He asked me what kind of peace I had found if it was so easily disturbed by how other people treated me. He teased me, asking me who did I think I was, the Princess of Zimbabwe? For the life of me I don't know why, but at the time that sounded very insulting! I do not remember much else of what he said. That question just kept playing over and over again in my head. But I do remember how it felt: I was so embarrassed. I was also angry and extremely humiliated!

I went home to my cute rented room and started packing my bags. I was furious, thinking I did not need to be around this old guy and his nutty students. Spiritual awareness, my ass! This place was a joke! Yes, as you can see I was very angry indeed. I am not sure which part made me angrier: having what I thought was a perfectly good question ignored, or that dreadful question "Do you think you are the Princess of Zimbabwe?" People were cracking up hysterically when he popped that question. Some laughed so hard they had tears in their eyes and were holding their bellies in pain. Hours later I could still feel the sting of embarrassment. I clearly did not get the joke!

When I calmed down enough to remember and reflect on what else he had said, I realized that he had made one good point. He asked me what I would do in life when people were not nice to me. Would people being nice to me be the only condition in which I could stay connected to my inner peace, joy and personal freedom? What kind of peace had I really found? How deep and how real was it?

My ego was infuriated because, I thought, "Well, I am not in the real world, am I? I am in a spiritual group with people who I thought should know better how to treat each other!" Wrong assumption!

The truth was that he was right. You can never escape human nature. As long as you are still living on planet Earth and humans are running the show, you will have to deal with their and your own fears, anger, envy, jealousy, rudeness, lack of tact and everything that can arise when humans gather together.

Having said how badly some of his disciples were behaving at times, when they were protecting their turf, they were also some of the most sweet, caring, open, fun-loving, passionate people one could ever meet! I can truly say we had some amazing times together celebrating and sharing wonderful, special moments. I had never received so much light and love in my life than I did with that group of people. So again, another great lesson learnt from that ego shakedown was this: on what did I want to put my focus? The bad behavior, or the good that was there in amazing abundance?! You could literally see the faces of new arrivals transformed from hard expressions of personal suffering into soft expressions of peace and deep joy. Yes, there was some ugliness in that group, but there was also so, so, so, so, much beauty and kindness!

Can you imagine surrendering your judgments, your anger, your ideas of how it's "supposed to be" and returning to a place where you feel you have lost face, a place where people may still be laughing at you because you seemed ridiculously stupid and funny in their eyes, your ego mask stripped away with nowhere to hide? Well, that's what it felt like to me all those years ago when I decided to stay instead of run away. It was a big victory against my ego; it was most humbling yet also very liberating.

I can truly say it was another turning point in my life, where knowing and living the truth became more important than feeding my insatiable ego. Papaji had given me a good kick in the butt, which was sorely needed! Lucky for me I could take it, and I used it as a springboard to dive deeper into peace, deeper than I had previously ventured. Not leaving Lucknow with steam blowing out of my ears was by far one of the best decisions I have ever made in my life!

His question was a good one. He really did get me – checkmate! "What will you do in life when people are not nice to you? Will you allow other people to dictate how you want to feel? Do not be so concerned about what other people are doing. Focus on yourself. Do not misunderstand me – it is good to care, but often we misplace this caring and make ourselves victims. Go deeper and find a peace that does not depend on the fickle nature of other people's moods, generosity or attitudes". I thought this was excellent advice. And I followed it. It is some of the best advice I have ever received.

Everything is intrinsically connected. There is nothing that exists on this planet that is not a part of you. Papaji taught me how to be at peace no matter what was going on around me, while also showing me that our human nature cannot be escaped. He was not a perfect man by any means, and neither did he claim to be. I believe that he and Osho made their mistakes too. They both had their own lessons to learn while living as gracefully as they could in their awakened states.

Papaji showed his transparency and willingness to be scrutinized by allowing us all into his private house. We could see him eating and sitting in his pyjamas watching TV and dealing with issues that made him happy and some that upset and angered him. This was truly a great part of the gifts he gave his students – his willingness to be seen offstage. He stripped away the option of our seeing him one-dimensionally as only a great teacher. He showed his own humbleness and egolessness by letting us know he was also just another fellow human being.

I now know I am not this body. I am not this mind. I am not what I own or what I do. I am that eternal energy that is timeless, formless and nameless. I am a love, peace and joy that knows no limits and is independent of what's going on in the world around me. This truth is not exclusive to me. It lies lost in every human heart, until that heart happens upon an experience good or bad which allows it to find its way back to itself. Turn your focus inward. Find out more about who you are, beyond the obvious things. Seek guidance along the path. Ask questions, be curious, meditate, contemplate, sit silently and connect to the silence and love the silence. Your questioning and your willingness to be with yourself in silence will lead you to the truth of who you really are.

It's that simple, and it's worth the effort. Like anything new, you are learning. The beginning requires a certain amount of commitment and then hey, before you know it, you are speaking French, eating escargots and French kissing. Or you are sitting silently, drinking in the silence and getting high on inner peace!

SECOND STEP: UNCONDITIONAL LOVE

Opening the Heart
Practicing unconditional love
Keeping a "pure heart"

You can't be on any kind of happiness quest without asking yourself if you are operating from an open heart, transparency and honesty. Being honest with yourself and others is something that you will need to work on vigilantly if you are sincere about accessing your greater Integrity.

The power to love and care profoundly is an instinct especially bestowed upon women because of the childbearing process they are capable of, while many consider men to have less of a connection to these qualities, apparently operating from a more insensitive and detached place. It has also been said by some that men lack intuition and that "sixth sense" that women are well known to possess. This all sounds to me like something the ego would encourage us to believe, to keep men and women on the warpath. Lord knows it is working! The ego battle between men and women is at an all-time high as women fight for their place out of the home. There is no doubt that men and women are different in many ways, emotionally and physically, but I personally believe that love, compassion and even intuition are qualities that both sexes can develop and be equally good at. This is because these qualities have a lot more than any other factor to do with what level of integrity and self-awareness each person operates from at any given moment.

The war for superiority between men and women is one that has been going on for a long time now, with some saying women are far wiser and superior to men on every level except brute strength. Others staunchly believe that a woman's place is behind her husband, letting him make the decisions and be the leader. What I find interesting is this: even while apparently being more intuitive and intelligent than men, according to some people's beliefs, women still have not yet found a way to take back the power from men and claim their obvious and rightful place as the better leaders.

I think I know why this has not happened. Maybe we women need to take a good look at what we are doing and see how we have contributed to and continue to contribute to the creation of some of the awful situations we have found ourselves in and continue to find ourselves in. Repression of women is a problem many women still face, many by choice, some against their will under pressure from their societies and even the governments under which they live.

When talking to women, I realize how we do seem to make bad decisions just as well as, if not better than, men! We date and even marry guys who do not respect us or value our contributions. We choose to have too many children when we do not even have the nerves, patience or resources for one. We remain in negative situations that go against our deeper truth. We do not love ourselves, nor do we respect our dreams. Of course there are many, many exceptions, so please do not take offence if you do not do any of these things. However, let us also not sugarcoat the emotional state of today's women.

If it were true that women are naturally superior and so much more capable of love and real compassion, then why don't they act more ingeniously? In some cultures, women have not even actively taught equality and fairness to their own male and female children. Why have they not protected their own daughters from harmful beliefs and rituals like circumcision of female genitals? These rituals can leave their own children maimed or even kill them. Some of these circumcisions have caused horrendous physical and mental suffering for those children for the rest of their lives. There are more examples one could present to argue against women's superiority over men, but I think you get the point! The ego, once again, is responsible for these horrible cultural beliefs that have been held for centuries, and are sadly still being practiced, even while it is clear that they lack anything which one could call compassion. Even calling it love is stretching the use of that term, in my humble opinion.

Maybe we all need to face the fact that when it comes to a higher self-awareness, women may be as lost as men. During childhood when their basic characters are being formed, we have taught, sculptured and molded the very men we accuse of lacking in sensitivity and awareness. Maybe we could have done – and should be doing – a better job at making sure that they stay in touch with qualities we appreciate, qualities like fairness, love, honesty, empathy, integrity. Most importantly, we should be teaching our children awareness of how their thoughts, words and actions will affect the lives of the people around them.

Women, it is essential that we acknowledge that we have made our contribution to what the world has become through what men have become. Do not misunderstand me. I am not saying that women have not been unfairly treated, abused and discriminated against. Sure, they have been, and the horror is that it's still going on in many places around the world. Yet we must think about how it may be that we have allowed and continue to allow it to happen.

If we want change and freedom, we must honestly see how we have contributed and continue to contribute to the situations that we so loathe. If you can change as an individual, you may inspire others to do the same. That's how we can make progress together. If we can revolutionize the way we educate our male children, maybe we would then see the rise of a better man. Then we might see more men we can respect and admire, not just as sons but also as husbands and leaders. Through working with women, I have come to see that we don't seem to have much respect for our men. The subject most women love to complain about the most is "men" and how they treat us. Ladies, we need to take responsibility for what we have created, and what we allow.

Even how we dress and treat each other does not help our case. Some of us walk around with most of our boobs showing, in super-short skirts where nothing is left to the imagination. Exposed bums, Botox faces and shoes so high and uncomfortable we can barely think straight. Granted, this may be a fun look at times. Yet, while presenting ourselves this way, we ask to not be treated as sexual objects. If we are serious about that, then we need to reconsider the direction our dress code is taking. Are we going too far down Sexy Lane? And does that affect how men see us and treat us today? Did we really fight for all this freedom so we could have the right to bare our breasts and bums to the world and not be called nasty names for doing so? I don't think so! Show less, ladies. That would be far more empowering and drop the "if you got it, flaunt it" perspective. Who are we kidding! But covering up in a burka is not what I am suggesting.

We need to work together to break free from the confinement of a male-dominated world. To do this effectively, ladies, you may have to open your minds to the fact that men may be a lot smarter than we give them credit for! Look how well they do for themselves. Men and women are on equal footing when it comes to harnessing our abilities to be generous, powerful, loving, open, creative, intuitive and compassionate. It's all just a question of what you have been taught and how you wish to evolve as an adult. The ability to love, be kind, and have integrity is not gender based. It's a choice that every human being makes based on the education from your parents, the society and any other strong influences you may be exposed to. You cannot truly evolve until you choose to set yourself free from these influences and dare to become "yourself" and an innovative free thinker.

I know that my mom dearly loved my sister and me, and yet I do wonder how she did not intuitively feel what was going on right under her nose. When thinking back on it, my sister had it written all over her face and attitude. Anyone could have noticed that something was just not right. My pill popping at fourteen was a cry for help that went unheard. I recall one particular birthday celebration where the whole family – Mom, Frank, my sister and me – went to a restaurant and my sister just sat there and cried.

I shudder to think how often women all around the world just fall asleep to their inner wisdom and intuition in exactly the same way my mom appears to have done. It's something worth considering, ladies. Are you right now "dumbing yourself down" in order to maintain a relationship? What would you see and what would you change if you decided to wake up, get empowered and acknowledge what's really going on in your life? You all have incredible access to greater intuition and clarity; however, you will need to own it! If guys are doing a good job at pulling the wool over our eyes, maybe it is because we allow them to get away with it!

Love Starts with You

Stop looking for a knight in shining armor for the fairy tale bride and real love will come into your life. If real love is to be found, you will have to find it within your own heart. When we love ourselves, not in an arrogant way, but in the purest way we can, we are at peace with who we are, warts and all. This kind of self-love will give you access to a greater empathy and compassion for other human beings too.

Having a healthy dose of self-respect and sense of wholeness in yourself will give you the strength to stay only in those relationships that serve the purpose of growth and learning for you and your partners, friends or family. Your relationship to yourself always needs to be more important than any other relationship. Some people might think this will make you selfish. Let me explain why I think it makes you the exact opposite.

Even your kids will be grateful to have a mother and father who take pride in their psychological, physical and emotional well-being and who do not lose themselves in their children. Getting overwhelmed, getting stressed out and out of balance, losing confidence, all happen because the parents forget to keep the relationship with themselves strong, healthy and happy. What child would not prefer a parent who is grounded in her or himself and knows how to be peaceful, joyful and present in the now? In order to achieve this you have to be willing to put your relationship to yourself above all other relationships.

It is more selfish to bring a child into this world and burden that child with your unhappiness, sadness, lack of clarity and involvement in unhealthy relationships. From this point of view it is a no-brainer, right? Stay connected to yourself regardless of what other relationships spring up in your life. Open your heart and practice loving yourself. This means being gentle, supportive and understanding with yourself, especially when something happens that triggers feelings of anger, frustration, sadness or any other negative emotion. These are the moments where your ability to remain loving, supportive and kind to yourself will be put to the test.

The more love and empathy you give yourself, the faster you will be able to let go of the negative feelings and thoughts that are haunting you. It's through the heart and not the mind that true passion and wisdom enter, live and grow in you. Stay present in the heart and you will access this knowledge much faster and not get stuck in misconceptions and misunderstandings, as easily as you could do using a mental approach to try to understand the deeper philosophies of self-realization. No matter how high your IQ, know that there is a part of self-realization which cannot be understood through the mind but only known and experienced through the heart.

How Do We Keep Our Hearts Open?

Sadly, we associate vulnerability with weakness, when it is in fact one of our greatest gifts as well as our greatest source of emotional strength. It keeps us soft and flexible, as opposed to becoming hard and brittle, mentally and emotionally. Anything soft and flexible like a rubber ball is going to survive better than something hard and brittle like a bottle. It would take a lot to destroy or put a dent in a rubber ball. We have all met hard and brittle people. That's what happens if you never allow yourself to show vulnerability and open mindedness.

Keeping an open heart is not as complex and difficult as you may think it is. The truth is always simpler than we are willing to accept. If you want to keep your heart open, then demonstrate accountability for how your thoughts, actions and words affect those around you.

You can start by closely observing the tone of the voice in your head. Loving yourself is vital when seeking the ability to be more peaceful and happy in the here and now, for the simple fact that you have to be with yourself twenty-four hours a day, seven days a week, 365 days a year. Even while sleeping, you still have to deal with yourself in the dream state. Trust me! If you continuously keep trying to avoid listening and being with yourself, your thoughts and feelings, this will only lead to trouble, or even illness. The sooner you turn this relationship into the greatest love story ever told, the sooner you can get on with enjoying more peace of mind in your daily life.

Not being loving and kind to oneself can lead to all sorts of physical and psychological problems, including eating disorders, depression, burnout, hypersensitivity, sleeping problems, backache and even hair loss due to stress. The list of horrors one can look forward to if one does not take care of oneself goes on and on and on and on, but I will stop here! When the physical or psychological health breaks down, this leads to a lack of confidence and to increased levels of fear, affecting your ability to perform well at work or in your personal relationships. Fear is debilitating and can lead to bad decision making, which can also lead to a whole host of other challenges. So understand just how important it is that you feel comfortable in your own skin and happy with who you are right now. We must keep our confidence levels high while remaining humble and nonegotistical. Sounds easier said than done? Not if you don't overthink it! You intuitively already know how to do this. It's just a question of getting on with it in your daily life.

The Voice in Your Head

I remember the annoying inner dialogue that would go on in my head before I found meditation. The self-loathing was as intense as the harsh criticism. I figured out that this was a habit I had picked up in my childhood. There was a lot of love in our family but also a lot of tension and fear. I can honestly say I don't remember receiving many compliments from family members during my childhood, except when I was dancing my little butt off! Most of the focus in those days was on what you were doing wrong, as opposed to what you were doing right. This taught me to do the same with myself. I am pretty sure most people have a similar experience of being taught to focus mostly on the negative aspects of themselves and of their lives. However, this is not an excuse for us to remain a victim of the past. Too many people use their past as an excuse to remain in suffering, and even to repeat, to some extent, the abuse they suffered. Sadly, they then end up passing the abuse on to their children. Get into the habit of continuously giving praise and compliments. Fill your world with enthusiasm and encouragement. This will help nurture positive self-talk in yourself and in the people around you.

Forgiveness

Fully give yourself to the practice of keeping a "pure heart". Do not be alarmed – I am not an old-fashioned puritan or anything like that! By pure, I simply mean a heart that is free from resentment, anger, fear or blame, towards yourself and other people. This includes people who have abused you, hurt you, broken your heart or simply did not care enough when they should have. The key to a pure heart is forgiveness. How do we get to the point where we can forgive something like abuse? I have, and it happened when I realized that holding on to the negative feelings and memories was only hurting one person – myself.

The person who has done something against you sadly did it out of his or her own deep lack of knowledge. Who knows what may have happened to them to cause them to stray off the innate path of their good nature? Who knows what abuse or horrors that person may have endured to get to the point of being totally lost and without a clear moral compass? I choose to believe that all humans are born as pure energy and love. It is what happens to them that will shape the basis of their character, and free will at one point will determine their actions and further crystallize their character.

To let go of resentment or sadness, we need to see that what has happened can never be changed. It's done. There is nothing we can ever do to alter that fact. Acceptance of this truth is a critical ingredient that will give us the strength to let go of the anger, frustration, or deep hurt and sadness that we may still be carrying around unconsciously. These unconscious feelings will affect your current relationships, so it is good to confront your past with an open heart, acceptance and forgiveness. It becomes a personal choice whether we will allow the past to continue disrupting our lives and limiting our ability to be happy and peaceful in the now. We can't control what other people do or did, but we can control how we react to their actions. Do not allow other people's actions and words to limit and define you. You are the only one who can allow that to happen.

We tend to blame people for our negative feelings like anger, sadness, frustration, confusion and so forth, when the truth is, we have the option to let go of these feelings and refocus our attention to feel whatever we choose to feel right now. Discovery of this truth was an extremely liberating moment in my life. To say it was empowering would be an understatement. If this is the only point you remember in this book, it will be a good one! You can choose where you put your focus, and that will affect how you feel. I choose to focus on the simple positive things in my life and in the world. I choose to feel happy and grateful. With this attitude, it is difficult for troubled feelings to linger for very long. When you start to focus on the good, the love and laughter in you, then those aspects expand and consume you. Through practicing self-love, acceptance and forgiveness, you will be learning how to love unconditionally.

What Do I Mean by "Practice Self-Love"?

I don't mean love, accept and respect only your physical body and your personality. I also mean respect and connect to that greater part of you. It is so important to include this in your self-image.

Most people don't give enough room for this part of themselves to express itself through the physical body. Their mind/ego has totally taken over the way they see and experience themselves. That's why everything feels so hard, looks so complicated and appears to be so challenging.

The moment you surrender your ego/mind to that greater part of you, the heaviness and sense of struggle in you will dissolve. That's when the feeling of lightness, trust and freedom comes into you. The only thing you are truly responsible for is your free will. Choose to be a happy, peaceful and loving human being. Everything else takes care of itself. I know this seems hard to believe, but this has been my personal experience for the last twenty years. It is as if being happy and peaceful makes you vibrate on a certain frequency, which the world around you responds to in a positive way.

Practicing self-love, which in turn leads to a deeper connection to unconditional love, will make you realize that inside of you is everything you will ever need to be happy in this lifetime. When you wake up to your inner strength, you realize you have been walking in the dark and suddenly the light is on. Before, you were falling over things and hurting yourself because you could not see the way. Now that the light is on, you can see everything. Love is like the spinach which Popeye, a hero from my childhood cartoon magazines, ate to gain increased powers to deal with the challenges he met along the road. Love will strengthen you in every way and take you beyond the limits you put on it. A heart full of love is indestructible! These are powerful statements that will start working for you if you take them to heart.

Self-respect and self-love will increase your peace of mind, as you are no longer fighting against yourself and being mean and impatient with yourself. Through meditation, contemplation, sitting silently and taking time out to reflect and quiet the mind, you will realize that the body is just a vehicle for something greater to express itself. That something greater is who you really are. That something greater is your limitless inner power. That something greater will allow you to go beyond your fear and self-doubt.

Overcoming a Broken Heart ♡

I know that anyone who has ever loved another has probably known the pain that comes from the beloved not loving you back or betraying you in a way you do not expect. It can feel like you will never love again or allow yourself to be that vulnerable. That would mean you are taking your first steps to becoming hard and brittle! Reflect deeply – you do not want to go down that path. Love is powerful stuff that should not be underestimated. It will allow you to forgive and let go of past hurt and heartache.

I remember the moment in my life when I really understood the meaning of unconditional love and what it means to keep an open heart. I was dating a Dutch guy. He was beautiful. Very tall, with sparkling blue eyes, long, thick blond hair and big red kissable lips. I was so in love. I liked everything about him, from his warm bubbling laughter to his sweet personality. He was the kind of person people just liked immediately. He enchanted old ladies and little kids alike. I was convinced that he was the one. As with Neo, "The One" in the movie *Matrix*, I had high hopes for this man. We dated intensely for about three months before he revealed to me that he had an ex-girlfriend whom he now knew he really loved and wanted to go back to. He also mumbled something about how they had not quite broken up, but had hardly seen each other since he and I had been dating. They were on some kind of timeout to find out what they really wanted and felt for each other.

I was really upset. It felt like a rude awakening and totally took me by surprise. It left me a moaning mess, curled up on the sofa for a few days. I thought obsessively about how he had betrayed and lied to me and made me fall in love with him anyway. I was disturbed and deeply hurt by the whole horrid business. During the first day or two that I was going through the breakup, I reflected a lot on what I was really feeling and tried to find the source of my pain. What exactly was making me feel so unsettled and miserable? I meditated, and the feelings would clear during the meditation, only to resurface shortly afterward. My experience over the years is that this only happens when there is some deep truth I am not facing, some gift to grow I am not receiving. Once you face it, you learn the lesson and the negative feelings dissolve as rapidly as they arose.

Some people think the only cure for heartache is time. Well, this is just not true. Self-love and facing the truth will also set you free and heal that broken heart faster than you could ever imagine. Recently I helped a lady through a breakup and she just could not believe how easily she was handling the whole thing. She felt empowered and in control and because she stayed in the heart, she did not experience the very strong, agonizing, painful feelings of rejection she had been fully expecting to feel. It was not even forty-eight hours after the rejection and she was laughing with her friends and getting on with her life again. She knows now from direct experience: you get more of what you focus on. She had kept her focus on the positive aspects of the situation. She had also chosen to continue to feel love and positivity towards the guy, and that was the real secret! That set her free from suffering.

So, back to my breakup story with the Dutchman demigod hunk! Somewhere on day three of the nightmare situation, I experienced a massive, life-transforming breakthrough. I realized that it was not love that was making me feel so bad, but the lack of it. Love in its purest form is unconditional and makes one feel nothing but pure bliss. Love does not belong to anyone: it cannot be given or taken away. It is as infinite as space and is not restricted by time. It's an eternal presence that does not begin or end at any point, like a circle. It's something that arises from the deepest part of our being. It needs no object to project itself onto. It can exist without provocation or cause.

It is without limits, except when the mind/ego gets involved. Then it mutates into this ugly thing that's clinging, insecure, unrealistic and a pain-feeding monster. We confuse our feelings of wanting to possess that person to being in love with them. Love brings joy and happiness to anyone who will truly allow it to embody them. When you see emotional suffering, know that it is caused by the lack of love in that situation. When you suffer badly in a relationship, it's not because you are so in love with that person. It's because you can't let go and love in the purest sense. You care more about your desires and the attachments rising from ego than the power, peace and freedom that comes with real unconditional love.

So, if you find yourself in a negative, unfulfilling relationship, crying out, "But I love him/her soooooo much! It hurts!" then stand to attention and pay attention. Look deeper into what's really going on and you will see the ego is messing with you again. It is making you think love is about pain and suffering, fighting and refusing to let go, even when it's clear that letting go is what you need to do to return to a happier, healthier and more emotionally balanced you.

I realized what it really meant to love someone. In my case, it was the tall Dutchman who unlocked the prison I had put my love into. He was still a two-timing bastard – no arguing about that – but he was also the guy that made me laugh and feel like I was floating on cloud nine. It feels good to love, so why separate yourself from it? It had been a fun ride until the rude awakening. Life had that extra glow of goodness. The air seemed that extra bit fresher and even the sun seemed to shine brighter. Those were still things, however, which I could always choose to notice and experience. So why would I have to stop loving him, or any other future partner, for that matter? Why should I have to give up this wonderful feeling of being completely and utterly in love? Who said love had to begin or end or belong to one person? Who said that because you could not own and possess someone, you have to stop loving them? Who said that because you can no longer make each other happy, you have to hate that person for failing? Who said that a lack of perfection in our partners is a good enough reason to hold on to feelings of disappointment and resentment? Nobody held a gun to my head demanding me to stick to these man-made rules about what is possible and what is not on the subject of love. So, I decided it was far less painful to forgive, let go, and stay with the energy of love in its purest form than succumb to the negativity of resentment and holding a grudge.

Through this breakup, I got the deepest insight into the real nature of love. The pain I was feeling about being betrayed and unloved disappeared. The Dutchman and I remained good friends. I wished him well and thanked him for the good times we'd had. I also advised him to practice more honesty and less selfishness in the future. Keeping me in the dark about the ex was not so cool! Ladies, can I get an "Amen!"?

I realized that love was something I had and could connect to inside me and not outside of me. My love was set free to run wild and uninterrupted. It was no longer dependent on what other people did or did not do. It is like a river that flows to become an ocean. The source of the river is inside me and through me the river flows out into the world, to become the ocean.

I realized that heartache did not have the same grip it used to have on me and the same drama I had attached to it. I had discovered the cure for heartache. The lethal and deadly weapon that stopped heartache dead in its tracks was love. Keep the love alive inside of yourself and let the relationship change as needed, to a friendship if possible, or a good memory if, for whatever reason, friendship is not possible. After all, it takes two to have a relationship. Every love story started with a connection to that real love inside us until the ego took over and wanted to possess it, own it, have it all for itself, and control it. Now, I can imagine some people wondering at this point – especially the women – "What exactly does she mean by this?" Am I saying we should all go out and have multiple sexual partners and forget about being in a monogamous relationship? For clarification, that is not what I am saying.

Relationship Tips

Being currently in a fourteen-year relationship, I can just share what I have learnt so far about how to marry truth with human relationships. It is important that you put your relationship with yourself and your peace of mind above that of any other relationship. That way you are not looking for the other person to fulfill your life. This means you will have a healthy self-confidence and take that responsibility upon yourself. This is essential for any strong, healthy relationship to be formed. With this attitude you will avoid the pettiness of jealousy or the overload of pressure that may come with being the centre of somebody's life. These things can destroy a relationship faster than most anything. That you love and accept yourself and value what you have to offer the relationship is important. Now, I am not saying that this means trouble-free times, every day of the year. It just means you will be sharing unconditional love as opposed to the possessive ego love. With my husband, Kai, I can honestly say that if our love were based in ego love, we would have already signed the divorce papers! When you are more in love with peace, happiness and the greater self than the relationship itself –

then you are setting up a relationship that's not likely to fail, really – and which can truly flourish. That's when things become really exciting, because the other person becomes a mirror for you to see your lack of connectedness to the limitless potential and love in you. Relationships offer endless opportunities to truly be yourself and access a greater kind of love.

We must give our partner wings to fly and be free, happy, full of passion and power. If we are always afraid that they will leave the nest when we give them full permission to shine and be themselves, then this is a recipe for creating and manifesting love that is only based in ego. If we prefer them to become dull and lose the spark that attracted us to them in the first place – so that no one will snatch them away from us – this cannot be good in the long run.

I don't mind when my husband looks at an attractive woman on the street. Hell, I too take double looks at any hottie. He is free to flirt shamelessly with beautiful women. I definitely want the freedom to do the same. With men, that is! Real love knows that it takes a lot more than an innocent flirt, a spontaneous stare, or even a hot dance to break the kind of powerful bond that is created when both partners practice unconditional love. It's tough work that not many want to do – to keep your relationship based in truth. That is why, in the end, so many relationships built on lies fail.

Sometimes we get stuck as couples. We take each other for granted and assume that we deserve loyalty whatever we do. But is this a very realistic point of view? I think loyalty should be earned every day. If we start to neglect the other person and stop communicating through the heart, maybe that is what will drive them to seek affection elsewhere. Once again, it's all about taking responsibility for what we create. If a partner has disappointed you on this level, maybe you need to ask how you took part in allowing this to happen. Experts in lie detection even claim now that we take part in the lie by allowing people to lie to us. That if we wanted to we could easily spot the lie and demand the truth.

I am always amazed at how many couples feel they can't talk openly about their sexual lives and true feelings to each other. There is much shame, insecurity and fear around the issue. It's such an important issue and can be a deal breaker if expectations are not met. So, it is important to deal with it in a full frontal manner. No sneaking around, looking at girls behind your girlfriend's back, or pretending to have orgasms you are not having! Have the courage to have an open, honest discussion, and if you want longevity in your relationship, keep having this conversation. When we stop communicating at some point, we usually also stop caring too, widening the gap and increasing the feeling of drifting apart.

Honesty is magical and positively transforming for couples when used with heart and willingness to be vulnerable. Make up new rules as you go along according to your individual characters and what feels right to both of you at any given moment. Do whatever you want to do, but be honest regarding your actions. Truth is very important because it gives us integrity and it is an ego destroyer. The ego thrives on lies, deception, smoke and mirrors – saying one thing but doing something else. We need to align our words with our actions if we are to know the true depth of our integrity and experience real trust. In my marriage, the truth keeps us open to each other and connected. With lies, we tend to drift apart. To become people of integrity is our noblest quality to master and embody. Frankly, it is really our greatest challenge! To conclude this step, let me remind you to practice self-love, unconditional love, total honesty and keeping a pure heart. It will make you a happier person.

FINAL STEP: KEEP QUIET
Keep Quiet – the Key to Letting Go

This is undoubtedly the greatest lesson I have learnt on my journey into the now. Papaji would say, "Mahima, just keep quiet. Whatever happens, just keep quiet. If something good happens, keep quiet. If something bad happens, just keep quiet".

This "keep quiet" technique made me truly realize the value of having a quiet mind. Our mind can hijack us into the past and into the future. The more present you are in the here and now, the less your mind can drag you around painfully. Putting this technique into practice is not as difficult as you may think. The secret is to just get started, and once you get over the first hurdles of practicing the skill to be quiet, you will love it.

The Observer

When we think about being quiet, a good place to start would be to literally practice more silence. First, spend time becoming fully conscious of how much you do actually love the sound of your own voice. During this time of observation, set a fixed goal period, like a week or two. Don't make any effort to change anything, just become more aware of how much you speak. Playing the role of the observer, carefully notice your words, actions and thoughts. Get to know your moods and attitudes more intimately throughout the day. When we are looking to transform our negative habits into ones that better serve us in our quest for happiness in the here and now, self-awareness is the first step. Look without judgment, but more with a curiosity to see what you can discover about yourself. You will be amazed at how easily you may lie to yourself or see yourself in a different way than others experience you. Ultimately it's more significant how we feel about ourselves than how others perceive us. This is because they are seeing us through the filter of their conditioning and their beliefs. Remember your opinion of yourself is the only one that really matters, because it is that opinion that will greatly affect your ability to be happy now.

After I took the time to observe myself without judgment, I discovered something really cool! That I am mostly good, with some bad habits, of course. Sometimes the very people (parents, teachers, etc.) that should give us the ability to believe in ourselves and see the good in us end up doing the exact opposite, keeping our focus on what's wrong with us rather than what's right with us. So be wary of other people's judgments of you and get to know yourself more intimately so you don't buy into their negative projections onto you.

Focusing on the Positive in You

Keeping quiet will allow you to start observing yourself and in doing so discover the positive in you. There is a positive part in all of us, no matter how buried below the surface it may seem. It is that part of us that makes us feel good and which instinctively knows right from wrong. Sages and philosophers refer to this positive part of us as our true nature.

What are you looking for during your self-observation experiment? You want to notice what kind of a mood you are in when you wake up in the morning. How do you treat the people in your life, even the stranger at the grocery store counter? Are you actually paying attention to people or just lost in your own thoughts? You want to become aware of how you treat your body. Do you mostly enjoy your work or do you hate every minute of it and count down the minutes before the next break or weekend? Are you able to enjoy your free time? Or are you still just working in your head long after you have left the office? Can you easily let go of negative thoughts and feelings? Do you find it easy to be in a positive mood? Or do you feel you are more stuck on a negative frequency most of the time? Do you bring joy to the people in relationships with you? Even work colleagues are in relationship with you. Are you so focused on the negative that all you can do is point out what they are doing wrong rather than what they are doing right? Yes, I agree, people do need to know what they are doing wrong, but if that's the only song you are singing, that makes for sad and exhausting relationships. You would do well to include the positive feedback, however small that may be. Those compliments or words of encouragement will go a long way in people staying open to your input. Focusing people around you on their positive qualities and contributions is what inspires them to want to be better and contribute even more.

Start practicing this with yourself. Focus on your positive qualities, see the good in you. Realize what your strengths are; compliment and encourage yourself. It's through self-awareness that the greatest transformation will take place. When limiting habits are brought into the light, they no longer have the strong power over you that they used to. Keeping them in the dark lets them thrive and strengthen their hold on you. So by getting to really know where your focus is, you empower yourself to change that focus to a more positive frequency. A good example is being a mean morning person. Is this a bitter pill those around you just have to swallow? Or is it time for you to see that this behavior is something you can let go of? What are you getting by holding on to this way of being? I can tell you, nothing positive. Don't be hard on yourself; if negative habits have taken hold of the way you live your life, just seeing this and having the sincere desire to be free to act differently is powerful stuff in itself. It is the bedrock of self-awareness that leads to personal development in a natural and easy way. The good news is that it is easier to free yourself from these habits than you may have previously believed – trust me. The secret is this: empower yourself by keeping your focus on the positive things that are in you and around you.

The Important List

So you have done your time of self-observation and now you have a more honest picture of how your personality interacts and deals with the world around you. Now what? Take a pen and paper and write down what you have observed about yourself. Don't hold back – be as generous as you can. Acknowledge the positive aspects of your personality. This list will crystallize and bring to life the things about yourself that you normally take for granted. Positive things in your personality that in fact are important anchors that will keep you positive on rough emotional seas.

Empower yourself by learning all your good qualities and learning to focus on them on a daily basis as well as put them into good use. Now do the same list with what you don't like about yourself. Don't hold back! Be honest but fair. Doing this will help you fully realize where there is room for improvement. Imagine if you are in an argument with someone and they accuse you of something like not being a good listener. If you have already admitted this to yourself, you can agree and try to do a better job next time instead of arguing and making the disagreement worse! The flip scenario would be knowing that you are a great listener and that that person is just projecting their negativity on to you. Know yourself intimately and honestly. Knowing yourself on all levels, plus and minus points, could actually help make your relationships easier and smoother.

Self-observation Period Completed

You have now spent time observing yourself, getting to know your habits and personality more intimately. You are hopefully starting to better understand the concept, "you get more of what you focus on". Where is your focus, in yourself and in the world? Don't forget that personality belongs only to the realm of the physical body. Our deeper nature is less individualistic and we are more similar to each other at the core. So do not get too hung up on trying to change your personality or drop bad habits – this will happen naturally as you hone your ability to keep your focus on the positive. This is an important point and where most seekers of peace and happiness in the now get stuck. Stop trying to change who you are in the now. Just concentrate all your vigilance on staying focused on the positive in you and in the world around you. The rest will happen by itself – trust me!

Now it's time to start keeping quiet and letting go. By understanding the concept "keep quiet", this will naturally lead you deeper into the heart of knowing how to let go. Being able to let go of negative thoughts and feelings is one of the most beautiful skills to master! It will naturally bring you deeper into inner peace in the here and now.

How to Keep Quiet

Start with the obvious by not having the radio or TV on as background noise at home or in the office, if that's at all possible. Turn it off when you are not watching it. Put the radio on when you are listening to it, or else it's just more noise in your already noisy world. Avoid always keeping yourself busy with an iPod, iPad or mobile phone. When you have free time on the train, bus or at home, try just sitting silently, doing nothing. It's becoming increasingly hard for people to connect with the idea of *just being* as our world hurtles along in fast-forward mode. We all try to squeeze so much into a day, an hour, a minute. The speed at which we move has become pure madness; even children are beginning to suffer from stress-related diseases.

Our days need silence injected into them, just as our bodies need fresh air gushing into the lungs and blood stream, just as water replenishes us and washes out toxins. The soul needs silence in the same way. That's why it feels so exquisite to be in nature because nature holds that transcendental silence as naturally as a mother holds her newborn baby. Allow silence to start working its magic on your body, mind and soul.

At first you might just hear the ravings of your mind at a louder volume. When we turn off the radio in the car on the way to work or when we turn off the smartphone, the emotional roller coaster of negativity may seem even more intense without anything to distract. This is a good thing, because we now we can become aware of what we are really feeling and thinking. It also opens the door for more inner peace and joy to enter into your life. When we allow more self-awareness to happen, this will bring positive results quickly.

Silence Brings Knowledge

When we allow high levels of unnecessary noise to surround us, we don't just block out the negative voice in our heads that we don't want to hear but also the intelligent wise voice that tries to speak to us through the heart. There is a profound wisdom that starts speaking to us from deep within the silence where our true power and potential lie. The outer silence creates a pathway to the inner stillness. Our minds and emotions can be brought back into balance by simply working with silence. As music or dance therapy can work wonders for people, silence holds even deeper properties to accelerate self-healing and promote self-development.

You have allowed yourself to be more submerged in the arms of the outer silence. Now it's time to literally start keeping quiet. This is the secret to letting the silence into you so you feel it more profoundly on the emotional and mind level. Whether you have a big problem or a small one, you will be amazed at what you can accomplish through just keeping quiet and reflecting in silence on the problem, allowing your inner wisdom to help you, listening beyond the noise of the ego mind and its limitations. Let's take as an example feeling stuck in a painful relationship. So many people come to me with this issue, and you may even know someone right now in that situation. A person can go on repeating to everyone who will listen how terrible their situation is. You may spend hours and hours doing this. Each time the complaint is repeated you give it more power and at the same time you lose power to act. With each conversation your emotions rise, intensifying and crystallizing in a negative direction. Most of the conversations you will have, sadly enough, will not lead you to find positive solutions. The discussions are more likely to lead you to increased negative emotions and feelings of hopelessness.

You may feel and think it helps you to share the problem, but actually this repeated sharing may end up contributing to the problem growing. Talking a lot can also contribute to sucking away the energy you need to do something about it. So it makes sense that if we would discuss less, we would also have more energy to contemplate on the issue more deeply and then take action.

When we talk to other people about our partners in a negative way, we increase our own negative feelings towards them. If you regularly engage in negative discussions about your bosses, family members, friends or partners, you give a lot of watering for those negative feelings to grow strong and healthy, making the gap between you and those people grow even wider. The same applies to anything we complain a lot about – our finances, our lack of this or that. My advice is, after you have told all your close friends once or twice about what you are feeling, it would be wise for you to just keep quiet and let your inner wisdom start speaking to you. This process of "keeping quiet" on the "issue" will put you in contact with different perspectives. Talking may be a way to avoid dealing with it all together. If you are not talking about it, you are processing it on a much deeper level and you will be amazed how quickly you move through the crisis or situation. Whether the problem is big or small, this keep quiet technique is powerful, and it works.

When you start practicing this technique, you will find that you won't need fortune tellers or other people to tell you what to do or what may happen if you do xyz. Your wisdom will be coming directly from the source and the person who knows you better than anyone else in the whole world – you. Learn to listen out for this inner voice, and never underestimate the power and clarity of your own wisdom and intuition.

The encounter with the tall Dutch guy brought the clarity that ultimately love has no beginning or end, but is more of a constant energy that is always present and available in the here and now. After I told my closest friends and family the sad story about the guy I loved who did not love me back, I knew what I needed to do next – just keep quiet! I knew from my other amazing experiences with this keeping quiet method that the letting go process would follow swiftly and sure enough, it did. When we give it space to enter into our lives, the silence will take hold and start to work its magic on us. That is what helped me to get that breakthrough. I started to question myself and look at how I could change my point of view to feel more positive and learn something from what was happening to me. I took responsibility for what I was feeling and stopped blaming him for what I was feeling. This empowered me and gave me freedom from the negative emotions that had wanted to continue hijacking me.

I saw clearly how it was my choice how long I was going to hang on to the negative emotions. Future hurt, frustration, heartache got treated with the same willingness to not blame someone else for what I was feeling. Silence is a powerful energy which can energize, rejuvenate and inspire greatness. Work with it. One could say that through my encounter with the Dutchman that I had struck personal development gold! I learnt how to deal with and let go of my feelings of betrayal and disappointment in a more positive and energy-effective way. Silence is a powerful teacher from which you will learn how to just let go and stay with peace.

If you feel stuck in a relationship, maybe there are even children involved and you just don't know what's the best next move. Try to start listening for your voice of profound truth and astounding wisdom that will speak to you through the sweet tender notes of inner stillness and outer silence. I have resolved countless inner conflicts this way and found the strength to take action in a positive direction, leaving behind discussions that lead to nothing, no change, no solutions, only more chatter and more negative feelings. This is a survival instinct worth developing.

For some reason we are more afraid of silence than ever: if there is even a small lull in the conversation, we tend to cringe and quickly try to fill the space with something, anything! I actually love when silence enters a conversation because from the awkwardness of that beautiful silence the truth is often exposed. Maybe it's best to end the conversation and stop beating a dead horse. Maybe the listener is just not that interested in the topic. Maybe the conversation takes a shift to a deeper level.

Fall in love with the silence in the way you love other things that bring great emotions into your life, like art, dance music, movies, hang-gliding, playing tennis or reading books. Silence will nourish your self-awareness and offer you room to reflect on your thoughts, words and actions. Introduce silence into the way you live – do not call it meditation! This might stress you out, and you will start thinking it's not for you. Being silent is not like yoga or any another hobby that suits some people and not others. It's like drinking water – everybody needs water, and the more you drink the better it is for you. I have great respect for this energy, as I have seen it working miracles in my own and other people's lives.

About twenty years ago, my crazy, beautiful sister asked me if she could borrow some money from me. She had found this solid deal that would guarantee at least 100% return on the cash invested within just a month! Anyone who knows my sister knows she is a very insistent lady when she is convinced about something. At the time it was impossible to say no to her. After the month turned into several months, it became obvious that there might be a big problem with the investment deal. When she started avoiding my calls altogether, it suddenly dawned on me that maybe I needed to accept that I might never see that money again. That somehow something might have gone horribly wrong, ahhhhhhhhhh! The amount was twelve thousand US dollars. It was the bulk of all the money I had at that time! After telling all my friends the story and getting super upset with my sister for blocking my calls and leaving me virtually penniless in India, I knew it was time to just keep quiet. I had almost spent all of the money I had not given her. Fear was swimming in my belly, greedily, trying to eat up all my feeling of calm!

A couple of days later, after I consciously decided to stop speaking about the awful position I now found myself in, from the silence a brilliant solution came to me. I got the idea that I could rent an apartment and make it fabulous using a very low budget and my limitless creative talents. I could then rent out the apartment for a price that could sustain my lifestyle in Lucknow. I calculated how much I would need to rent the apartment for, to allow extra cash to pay my own rent and daily expenses. The numbers added up and my plan could work, but only if I found the right apartment.

No sooner had the solution popped into my head than some hours later I heard someone saying they were leaving and wanted someone to take over the renting of their apartment. Yeah, it's hard to believe, but it's true. My eyes nearly bulged out of my head when I saw the place! It was perfect! I needed so much control to not break out right there and then into a happy dance, hammer style, especially after they told me the rental price which, for some reason, was insanely low! I still negotiated on it though, as it was the custom to do so, plus hey, I was the closest I had ever been in my entire life to zero. And it was way too close for comfort. The location of the apartment was just walking distance from the meditation hall and it did not need much work or money to turn it into a stunning oasis.

I honestly could hardly believe my luck. This continued a few days later when the universe presented me with someone who loved the place and wanted to rent it for half a year! Within a week of starting to use the keep quiet technique, I had found a solution. They paid me in cash up front for the whole six months. This is, to me, as close to a miracle as one ever gets. Engaging this technique has created countless miracles in my life of similar effect over the years and years I have worked with it. Sometimes problems get solved faster than I can say, "Houston, we have a problem!" Sometimes one just needs a little more patience and trust, but it has not yet let me down.

Keeping quiet combined with letting go is a powerful cocktail. I could have totally freaked out at the idea of not having any money!

Final Step: Keep Quite

After I downed this "cocktail", I consciously chose to meditate, to stay calm and focused on the positive that is in me and around me at all times. I chose to remain present, open hearted and open minded to what would happen next. I trusted that I would find a solution. I remain amazed at how well this method of solving problems works.

My sister took about eight months to pay that money back to me, and when she did, she gave me back twenty-five thousand US dollars instead of the twelve thousand she owed me! Yes, I know! Who does that when they do not have to?! That was extra cash I was not expecting and to be honest with you, I had already written off the other cash too – I had just meditated and worked on being happy in the now. I can tell you it was a glorious thing to actually see all that money in my bank account. It was like a deep acknowledgement in what I had come to believe – when you focus on positivity you get more of that in your life. It's that simple.

My sister, it must be said, is an amazingly generous human being, helping so many people, from family members to total strangers. She goes above and beyond the call of duty when it comes to her financial and emotional generosity, a true example of an angel on earth, touching and enhancing other people's lives in a positive way. She is certainly a great role model in my life. She gracefully managed to turn her adversity into fuel and passion for her personal development. She continually amazes me!

The whole situation taught me so much about trust and how we get more of what we focus on. When we can just keep quiet, let go and see how the things play themselves out, we start to realize just how much energy we waste worrying, fretting, jumping to conclusions, over analyzing and most amusingly, trying to cross bridges before we even get to them. Things are not always as they seem, so try not to jump to conclusions. Resolve to stop, breathe deeply, keep quiet, keep an open peaceful mind and just let go rather than entering states of prolonged high drama, anguish or negative emotional chaos. Life will present many opportunities for you to put this wonderful step into practice, so if you put your heart into mastering silence, you can become good at it – in no time at all.

If you are serious about wanting personal freedom from unhappiness and confusion, then please invite silence into your life and into the way you deal with problems, and you will see results and maybe even a few quantum leaps into a more peaceful, powerful you. By the way, less than two years after being rejected by what I thought at the time was the love of my life, I met an even more awesome man, my husband, Kai. This relationship has far surpassed all that I wished for, and trust me, I wished for a lot! If I thought the other guy was cool, I had no clue, really. He was lovely, but Kai is in another league completely. I thank my lucky stars every day. The point I want to make is this: just keep quiet, watch, learn and try to stay calm and open hearted and open minded no matter what life throws at you. You never know how things are going to turn out in the end. Bad may turn out to be good and what you thought was good may turn out to be fanfreakingtastic! The universe wants us to succeed – we just need to trust.

Letting Go

Letting go is all about taking responsibility for where you choose to put your focus. What you say and do or don't say and don't do. Who you allow into your inner circle and how you choose to spend your precious time on this planet. The one thing I have witnessed over and over again as I work with people to assist them to find peace in the here and now is the lack of willingness to be fully responsible for their choices. It's like the line between childhood and adulthood has not been fully understood, accepted and crossed over. Sounds harsh? Let me explain.

When we were children, we were pretty helpless and choiceless. We needed to be fed, bathed and we even needed someone to wipe our bums for us. As we grew older most of us could start to do that and other things on our own. However we pretty much had to accept and follow our parents' rules whether we agreed or disagreed with them. They chose our religion, our schools, our clothes and even the way we wore our hair. This may be light years away from today's kids, but at least this is how I was brought up! Parents also tried to choose our friends, approving of some and disapproving of others. They taught us how to do just about everything, even controlling the language we use and the way we speak.

Our parents and society molded us into young adults. By the time we could decide for ourselves, we were too busy trying to be who they wanted us to be. It could be that we have forgotten to cut the invisible umbilical cord that we formed to them and make that all-important transition from feeling helpless to feeling empowered. This is a serious point I really I would like you to consider. I see so many adults who blame others for their bad feelings, and family is often on the top of that blame list. Growing up and empowering yourself is about fully engaging your free will, a free will that slowly developed along with learning to walk and talk as we grew taller and stronger. The ability to make choices – that's all free will is. We make choices every day that affect how we feel and what might happen to us.

If you are willing to take full responsibility for your choices, you will start to tap into your incredible inner strength and feelings of empowerment. You will start to live in a reality where you feel more in control in the here and now. Letting go of negative emotions like sadness, anger and fear is a personal choice you can make every minute of the day. You can engage your choice, your free will, to stop, breathe, keep quiet and let go of negative emotions by choosing to focus on the positive ones. However bad the situation is, there are always two sides of that coin. Which side do you wish to put your focus on – the plus or the minus?

When I decided to grow up and fully accept that I was not just a victim of my circumstances but also very much a creator of my daily reality, I empowered myself, and my life really did become more joyful. It became joyful because I realized that the secret to my happiness really did lie within my ability to make better choices and choose consciously to not give fuel to negative feelings and thoughts.

I did a big spring cleaning in my life and felt wow! I am finally growing up and it feels good. I reexamined some relationships and decided what role I wanted them to play in my life. As a child you are pretty helpless in choosing your relationships. This is one of the greatest perks of adulthood. Choose your inner circle wisely! Surround yourself with positive, loving and supportive people.

As an adult you decide how you want to do things and which road you want to take. You decide what is possible and what is impossible. You set the boundaries and you set the limits. You decide how far you will go and when to quit or change lanes. Ah, the joys of being an adult! Have the courage to be authentic and carve out your own path. It can be a path which no one you know has ever dared to go down before or a well-known and well-used path. Either way, it's your choice. It's not luck.

Now that's all the obvious part, and I am sure everyone has had or will have that growing-up moment in their life. However, we must go deeper, liberating ourselves from negative influences and beliefs that our parents and the society have taught us.

Beliefs Are Powerful Things

Our beliefs are powerful things that can imprison us or set us free. Become conscious of how yours affect your behavior and thought patterns.

An example I can give you is this: I grew up in a country where racism was a way of life, and most people indulged in it. Not only blacks against whites, but Indians against blacks, and coloreds against blacks, whites and Indians! As part of my spiritual spring cleaning when I realized it was time to grow up, I recognized there was some racism and prejudice in me. It was not strong and all consuming, by any means, but it was there, hiding cleverly behind excuses and logical arguments, a subtle ugly energy that made me judge people without getting to know them or gave me a warm glow of arrogance around certain people. I definitely needed to watch a tendency to want to jump to conclusions about people because of their appearance, social standing or level of education.

I did not like this in me, so I put it on my list and observed it. It was learnt behavior from my family and society. During my childhood it was common for adults in my family to use derogatory words against other races. It is best at this point if I do not go into details!

Let your imagination run wild and free! These things affect us and even if we think we have escaped being the same as those who taught us, we have to work to make sure that is really true.

Where could you change your attitudes and ideas that were taught to you but don't necessarily serve the higher qualities of integrity, love and peace? It's important to recognize where we may just be going through the motions, like feeling warm in the arrogance of feeling better than our parents while in fact we are not really being that much different from them. We all like to think we are good people and don't need to bother to actively work on being better people. This is a typical ego point of view.

I personally believe we are all subtly racist and prejudiced to some degree and of course some of us less subtly. We must first admit it to ourselves in order to truly transcend it and start treating others with the fairness and courtesy we wish to receive. The only way you could have totally avoided having some sort of prejudice or racism is if you were born and bred on another planet! Please treat this subject with as much integrity and honesty as possible instead of outright denial and lack of accountability. This way we can start to truly make progress as we look to bring economic and spiritual peace to more places in this world. Start with bringing better attitudes around this subject to your own neighborhoods and businesses by encouraging and embracing diversity.

Being an extraordinary person is about having the courage to admit to yourself where you could be better and then getting on with it! Start listening to the conversations going on around you. You might be surprised what you will hear when you take time to just listen as a neutral observer to what people are saying and how they are saying it. You will start waking up to the truth of what's really going on, as opposed to living in the lie of what you hope is going on around you. Aspire every day to be better, stronger, wiser and calmer. Silence will help you to do this. You have a free will – use it wisely to start building a community of wonderful, loving people around you. Lead by example. It's like recycling – the more everyone takes part, the greater good we shall do for this planet. The more people increase their levels of integrity and joy, the more powerful the effect will be on the future we are currently creating by our actions in the now.

Old Wisdom

There is great wisdom in the old scriptures and books but also ideas that create much separation and suffering among us humans. We must own this to move forward in a more positive way. Take the knowledge that rings true to your heart and have the courage to reject everything else. We need to treat each other more respectfully, and religion, sadly and ironically, sometimes does not allow us to do that!

In all religions today there is a great amount of wisdom and also many outdated ideas and concepts. Do you have the courage to look at what might be outdated or conflict-generating philosophies in your religion? Why are we still so concerned with what somebody did thousands of years ago to help us understand what we need to do today? The worst thing is that those books have been around for so many thousands of years and yet we still do and have done horrible and even unthinkable things to each other. Massive world wars, slavery, disempowerment of women – just to mention a few of the "great things" we have done while totally under the powerful influence of religion. Maybe one of the worst things we have done is set up a system that keeps others in poverty and filth while others prosper and enjoy extraordinary wealth and riches. Did you know that about 85% of the world population is religious? Make no mistake – its influence on us may seriously be part of the slow evolution in human compassion! There are obvious limits to its ability to help us truly come together as one human race, standing alongside each other instead of fighting. Respecting instead of fearing each other.

Some may argue that greed and power is responsible for this division and that this lack of unity among men is not at all God-related. I would argue that for centuries, all around the world, almost all politicians have belonged, with great passion and gusto, to some religious group. Yet their ability to unite us in our love for each other and this planet is still light years away from where it needs to be, so that all may flourish and economic fairness, spiritual harmony and balance rule planet Earth.

When it comes to our religions, all reason and common sense seems to go out the window! However, let's not linger too long on the side effects of being a nation still strongly hooked on the religion drug. Let's rather focus on the positive – that you are reading these words and you will hopefully allow yourself to dare to question your religion much, much more. Not only the ancient texts or the priests, monks, rabbis or other religious leaders, but also yourself.

It is my hope that in the power of this questioning, you can free your mind and heart from any petty and cruel thinking and from following sheepishly and blindly. And also from allowing things to continue that you know deep down inside should have stopped a long time ago.

People believed that the world was flat until it became common knowledge that it most certainly was not. Does God have to have one name or face? What old archaic ideas do you cling to that would do us all good if you let go of them? In the silence, you will talk less and listen more. You will have time to reflect not only on what you might eat for dinner tonight but also on the deeper questions that we really must ponder. We must do this if we are to reach far beyond what we already know. Questions like, Who am I? Do I practice unconditional love? Do I judge people by the way they look or their status? What energy am I vibrating on and putting out to the world around me? What role do my beliefs play in what I am creating in my daily life? Is happiness a gift bestowed upon a lucky few, or a personal choice? What can I do right now to change direction onto a more positive route?

You will need the silence to contemplate and reflect on these things throughout your lifetime. We have this brilliant mind which is there not just to remember where we live and what our name is. It's there not just to allow us to learn to be a great doctor or a businessman – it can also be used to focus, discover, explore and uncover the deeper essence of our true human nature, a nature that will allow us to experience a peace and love that knows no limit except that which we individually impose on it.

Courage to Fly Out from the Nest

We can learn a lot from teachers, but we can also easily get stuck on the teacher trip. At one point on your journey you will need to give up the teacher-student relationship in order to take that last step into freedom and live your own truth. Now, I don't mean that you have to start bad-mouthing or rejecting your teacher in any way. That would be ridiculous and lack integrity. I have seen some people get so frustrated with themselves that at one moment they did just that. With this action, they also throw away the years of good work they may have done with that teacher.

What I mean is that in order to grow stronger and clearer, we have to be willing to cut the umbilical cord that has nourished us with knowledge, love and energy. To cut the cord is a conscious decision you will have to make and know when to make. You will have to overcome your own self-doubt and the doubts of people around you. Others people around the teacher will frown upon you when you do this. They may even say it is impossible for you to have reached the same state of deep awakening as the teacher has. This may or may not be said directly in words, but their actions and the way they treat you will speak this message loud enough. This belief in teacher supremacy limits many followers and that's why even after many years of meditation some people can still feel stuck in personal suffering. They are stuck in the teacher trip and the enlightenment trap. They have put their teacher on such a high pedestal that they can no longer see that the teacher is only a mirror. They have given their power away. Sadly, many people have the wrong idea of what it means to be awake and foolishly hope awakening will free them from their human nature.

To feel that the teacher is wiser and knows more than you is a correct perspective when you first arrive in the teacher's presence to learn and develop. There is a moment, however, when the teacher has helped you all he can to absorb his knowledge and everything that has been said. Everything has been given, experienced and understood beyond the mind. This is the moment to step away and allow your own inner guru to take over. If one does not recognize when this point comes, they can get stuck in concepts of the mind, ideas and beliefs about freedom that have nothing to do with being peaceful, loving and content in the here and now.

Having spent so many years around seekers, I witnessed what happens when people miss this point and restlessly run after more and more and more of what they cannot quite say, but they believe exists. They struggle to understand and take this last step: owning your freedom, taking full responsibility for yourself and becoming your own teacher. Putting into practice every day everything that has been learnt – bringing that wisdom into your every step, breath, word and action.

It is the last step every man or woman who claims to be free has taken. With the right teacher, the awakening is the easy part. Living from that truth in a world that is doing the opposite is the most interesting, exciting and somewhat challenging part. That is the part that may cause doubt about how easy it all is! That is why it's good to have a guide and strong leader along that path. That is also why I would always go away from Lucknow for months at a time. I was developing that relationship with my own inner guru. By the time

Papaji died, my inner guru happily stepped into his shoes. Years before he died, Papaji encouraged me to start sharing meditation sessions with other people. I had no idea where to start, but I knew that it would become clear when the time was right, so I just went about my business. When he died, I knew I was ready. I knew the time had come to spread my wings and fly out of that wonderful cozy protective nest of the teacher-student relationship. It was time to take that last step into true freedom.

Once I had made the decision, I flew from New York to Bali and was offered the chance to share my knowledge in a beautiful retreat centre in the hills of a small city on the north side of the island. Once again everything fell into place beautifully. That one meditation session snowballed into a series of invitations to teach all over Europe. I found myself giving sessions in various cities in France, Switzerland, Belgium, Holland and Germany. I was amazed how it took on a life of its own. I can truly encourage anyone to dare to follow your true passion. Follow your heart, not your head. Follow your dreams and don't settle and do not give up on them, whatever happens. You will be wonderfully surprised at how things have a way of turning out even better than you imagined when you stay positive and present in the now.

EPILOGUE

Everything you need to be happy is inside you

Once you can truly embrace this concept, it's happier days from there on out! What makes us suffer is that we look to fill the feeling of emptiness and pointlessness. We look for love in others when it is in us. We look for respect and kindness from others when we don't even give it to ourselves. Our focus is on the negative while so much beauty is inside us and around us. We don't want to take responsibility for how we feel. We would rather just blame someone else for our negative feelings.

We lack integrity and have prejudices against people who are different from us but convince ourselves that we don't, while our actions sadly reveal the truth. Some of us have everything we could possibly need and more to be as happy and as free as a bird in the sky, and yet we can't stop complaining or shake the feeling that something is missing. We think it's right to put work obligations before our family's emotional needs and our love relationships instead of finding a way that brings joy to both work and play.

We are spoilt for choice, and yet it's never enough. We are lost in our egos that hide us from the truth, yet we don't recognize that we are lost. We think we have time when it's clear that the only time we have is this moment. We spend so much time crying over spilled milk and fretting about the future even while the moment holds the solution to our peace of mind.

We trash the planet with our greed for money and power, yet we cry for the poor people that suffer. We see the imbalance but find no lasting solutions. We pray to God to forgive us rather than just be responsible for our actions. We think love is owning and controlling somebody and clipping their wings so they can't fly off. Some people don't speak to their ex-partners anymore and yet they are trying to teach their own children about love and forgiveness.

We treat each other with contempt and lack of trust or care but expect people to like us and treat us with respect. We blame the world for what we are feeling when we do nothing to feel better. Some people might read these words with frustration, some amount of anger and perhaps even a fair amount of denial.

Yet if we could just accept our failings, we could start the process to truly rise above and become better human beings. Self-awareness is the first step. We must claim our current reality in order to rise above and realize our incredible beauty and inner light.

We must be willing to face the truth of what we have been, the truth that we are and the truth that we shall become when we continue down the course we are on. Stop, breathe, relax and start heading in a new direction, a direction that celebrates diversity, working together, stopping killing and fighting. A direction that teaches unity, sharing and harmony. I have had many discussions with many people from all walks of life, and sadly, I see denial eating away at most people's ability to act with greater self-awareness and human compassion. All the goodness is there inside us, that is for sure – we were born with it. We just need to have the courage to reach out for it and give that aspect of us greater space in our everyday lives.

Master the ability to treat yourself with love, kindness and respect. Then move on to practicing this on the people around you. Be a good leader and lead the people around you to be better, kinder, more peaceful and happier human beings. Make it your life mission to be a person of integrity. Let's stop pointing fingers in all directions and just start working on ourselves.

It will take all your heart and dedication for this idea to succeed, the idea that one person – you – can make a big difference in many people's lives. Sometimes it will just be a warm smile you give to a lonely stranger, or some greater act of kindness that will elevate the lives of the people around you.

You can make a difference. You are amazing. You are strong and powerful. You have a limitless goodness and energy within you. Dive inward, find that truth inside yourself and have the courage to start living it in your daily life, even if it goes against everything you have ever been taught or conditioned to believe is possible.

In every human heart lies a smoldering fire and desire for peace, love and happiness. When the right wind blows, that fire can become a bonfire that burns everything else which is not true in an individual, everything that holds you back or obstructs your inner light from shining brighter than the brightest star in the universe. Ask the question "Who am I?" The answer will liberate you from suffering. Practice unconditional love: love yourself and you will love the world and life will be more magical. Keep quiet and you will gain access to immense wisdom and life-transforming power. Three simple powerful steps to a happier you.

Now stop, breathe, relax and love silence!
It will make you happier.

Mahima Lucille Klinge

67949169R00113

Made in the USA
Columbia, SC
03 August 2019